Also by Jane Garmey
Great British Cooking: A Well Kept Secret

Great New

SIMON AND SCHUSTER·NEW YORK

British Cooking

JANE GARMEY

The Decorations by
Christopher Wormell

Simon & Schuster Building
Rockefeller Center
1230 Avenue of the Americas
New York, New York 10020

SIMON AND SCHUSTER and colophon are registered
trademarks of Simon & Schuster, Inc.

Designed by Barbara M. Marks
Manufactured in the United States of America

1   3   5   7   9   10   8   6   4   2

Library of Congress Cataloging in Publication Data
Garmey, Jane.
Great new British cooking.
Includes index.

1. Cookery, British.   I. Title.
TX717.G33   1985   641.5941   85–14287
ISBN: 0–671–53258–8

For
Monica, Rachel and Rosemary

Contents

Acknowledgments

This book could never have been written without the gracious cooperation of the many British chefs and cooks who so generously shared their recipes with me. I would like to thank all of them and also extend special thanks to Peter Herbert and Kit Chapman, who went out of their way to provide me with valuable assistance. My thanks also to Peter ffrench Hodges and Bedford Pace, who were both endlessly helpful and sent me off in good directions; Sue Newall, who kept me abreast of her culinary discoveries; Maxine White, who was an indefatigable eating companion in England on even the hottest days; and my husband, Stephen, indispensable reader and eater-in-chief. Finally, I would like to thank Carole Lalli, whose idea it was to do this book and who quite literally talked me into the doing of it.

Introduction

Not so many years ago one would have been hard pressed to find an English country restaurant offering anything like a chicken liver terrine with Cumberland sauce, roast duck stuffed with black currants accompanied by tiny broad beans and new potatoes, summer pudding—bread soaked overnight in a mixture of raspberries and red currants, its red juice deftly traced with delicate circles of whipped cream—and an array of cheeses that included a Blue Vinny from Dorset and a Cotherstone from Yorkshire. And yet I recently sat down to exactly that meal in a small hotel dining room in the depths of the English countryside.

My pleasure at being served such a feast was mixed with real surprise, for I confess to a long-held prejudice—based on painful experience—that cooking of this kind was seldom if ever to be found in a British restaurant, let alone one outside of London. My surprise was compounded when, in the space of a two-week period, I found other meals of the same quality and standard in different parts of the country—meals that included fresh local produce and were prepared by chefs who combined sophisticated cooking skills with a willingness to use traditional ingredients in new and imaginative ways.

Up until that time, I had always felt that eating out in England was a risky enterprise at best and one that usually entailed any number of hazards. To begin with, most restaurants served only "foreign" food prepared by persons who had never been abroad. The menus themselves were pages long and always written in a foreign language. With very few exceptions, the food was overcooked, tasteless, invariably overpriced and usually bore little resemblance to whatever original creation it purported to be. For some reason I never understood, the kind of British food *I* liked—local fish, stews, meat pies, root vegetables, syllabubs, fruit tarts and fools— was never to be found on any menu. It was eaten only at home, a native cuisine that remained a well-guarded secret behind closed doors. I have always been convinced that one of the reasons for the legendary unpopularity of British food in this country is that most Americans have had the misfortune always to eat out in Britain and rarely in.

But here in a little country hotel was something different; my theory was falling apart. Clearly, change was afoot and I needed to reassess my thinking. I had heard reports that a new British cuisine was indeed making its appearance, but I wanted to see for myself. My journey took me to the hotels of certain young British chefs who had recently formed a group called Country Chefs Seven. This had allowed them to get together on a regular basis, exchange ideas and recipes, discuss common problems and, of course, eat. It also allowed them to announce to the public that this emerging group of young British chefs (with not a French accent among them) took their profession very seriously and were both skilled and talented. Their organization, it turned out, was symptomatic of the considerable change of culinary climate taking place all over Britain.

Since that visit, I have been converted and everywhere I see signs of change. Not only has London reestablished itself as a great city in which to eat, some of the best food is also to be found outside of London, in a series of impeccably run, small and extremely comfortable country house hotels (in the United States they would be called inns). These hotels are most often converted manor houses, elegantly appointed with antiques, fresh flowers, down pillows. Their owners are not interested in annexes or expansion; their attention is directed to comfort, service, wine lists and, above all, good food.

At the same time there is a growing interest in cooking and eating from a more critical and better informed public, a willingness to experiment and try new dishes, a realization that good cooking does not need to be overly complicated and a recognition that local fresh ingredients are always preferable to fancy, frozen imports. Menus are now being written in plain English and this is happening not just in small restaurants but even in such "continental" bastions as the Ritz. And, whereas food never used to be considered a fit subject for conversation, now the talk is all of food— where to find Marin eggs, chanterelles and unpasteurized farmers' cheeses. Like any new movement, there are of course excesses and a certain preciousness; and overdependence on the tenets of nouvelle cuisine sometimes tends to rub one the wrong way. In spite of this, however, it is a healthy movement and one that in many ways parallels the kind of gentle revolution that is now going on in the United States.

This book is my attempt to bring American readers a sampling of some of the new recipes I have come across in Britain and to give some sense of the variety of food that one can find there today. It should not in any way be considered an inclusive picture of contemporary British food or British chefs. Many excellent restaurants are not represented here. Some were frankly too grand; others I discovered, unfortunately, too late to include. This is a subjective collection which also gives some of my own recipes and those of friends and acquaintances. My hope is not only that readers will be encouraged to try out some of these recipes but also that this book will lead them to many of the hotels and restaurants mentioned when next they visit Britain. Then they too will find that it is at last possible to dine very well there, even when eating out.

Soups

Where better to start than soup? Comforting on a cold winter's night yet equally good, served cold, as the beginning to dinner on a summer's evening. Soup is nothing if not versatile and, thanks to the invention of blenders and food processors, it can be extremely simple to prepare.

For a long time, many of the best traditional British soups were those least likely to appear in public—hearty soups with root vegetables such as parsnips or turnips as their base. Long exiled to the nursery and the kitchen, they are now at last beginning to make their appearance in the upstairs world.

Other developments in the British kitchen include the proliferation of curried soups, many of which draw their inspiration from that traditional colonial classic, Mulligatawny soup. Cheese-based soups are also becoming popular. One of the best Stilton soups I have tasted comes from Michael's Nook in Grasmere.

Soups

Winter Soups

New Season's Fragrance
Hot Cider and Onion Soup
Turnip and Scallion Soup

Mustard and Mushroom
Soup
Curried Parsnip Soup
Welsh Leek Soup

Fish Soups

Curried Fish Soup
Smoked Haddock and Leek
Soup

Water Souchet
Mussel and Saffron Soup
Oyster and Guinness Soup

Summer Soups

Chilled Gingered Carrot
and Orange Soup
Pea, Lemon and Mint Soup

Cream of Celery and
Stilton Soup
Saffron and Leek Soup
Curried Apple Soup

Winter Soups

New Season's Fragrance

This exceptionally delicate and delicious consommé comes from Nick Gill, the very young, talented chef at Hambleton Hall. Set on a peninsula in Rutland Water, near Oakham, Hambleton Hall is one of the best of all the English country house hotels and has become one of the most desirable escape points from London. Just under two hours of driving brings one to an elegant nineteenth-century house filled with antiques, fresh flowers, down pillows and books in every room. The hotel is owned and managed by Tim and Stefa Hart, who follow one simple, unencumbered rule: provide the very best. Nicholas Gill falls into that category and the food he serves is superb. However, good food does not necessarily need to be complicated and this recipe is a case in point. But don't attempt to make this soup unless you have two chicken carcasses on hand, as the strength and freshness of the stock are the key to the taste of the soup.

2 *chicken carcasses*
2 *carrots, finely chopped*
2 *medium-sized onions,*
  coarsely chopped
2 *stalks celery, finely diced*
2 *leeks, washed, trimmed*
  and sliced
2 *cloves garlic, chopped*

3 *tablespoons chopped*
  parsley stalks
2 *bay leaves*
½ *teaspoon thyme*
1 *egg white*
¼ *pound smoked chicken*
1 *bunch fresh basil*

Place the carcasses and the carrots, onions, celery, leeks, garlic, parsley stalks, bay leaves and thyme in a three-quart saucepan. Add eight cups of water and the egg white. Bring to a boil, cover completely and simmer gently for 45 minutes, stirring from time to time.

Strain the stock carefully through a double thickness of muslin or cheesecloth into a clean saucepan. Cut the smoked chicken into thin matchsticks and shred the basil leaves.

Divide the consommé into separate cups or bowls and add some of the chicken and basil to each portion. Cover each cup with a piece of foil and place on a cookie sheet in a moderate oven for a few minutes so that the consommé can be served very hot. Allow each person to take off the foil cover from his own portion in order to unveil the special fragrance of this soup.

4 TO 6 SERVINGS

Hot Cider and Onion Soup

Michael Quinn is an ebullient, bearded Yorkshireman who until recently was head chef at the Ritz in London—the first Englishman ever to hold the job at the 80-year-old hotel. Making changes at the Ritz, where the memory of Escoffier is still sacred, was no easy task. However, Quinn seems to have thrived on challenge and he ushered in the winds of change— the enormous menu has been pared down and is now written in English, the vegetables are never frozen, the dishes are more seasonal and there has been considerable infusion of young blood into the kitchen staff.

This recipe, which is very filling and quite delicious, comes from Michael Quinn. Serve it with a salad and cheese and it will make a complete meal.

5 *large onions, finely*
   chopped
8 *tablespoons unsalted butter*
⅔ *cup flour*
6 *cups chicken stock*
2 *cups country cider*
1 *bouquet garni (thyme,*
   bay leaf and parsley)

½ *cup heavy cream*
1 *apple, peeled, cored and*
   cut into thin segments
1 *cup toasted croutons*
¾ *cup grated Gruyère cheese*

Cover and sweat the onions in one-third of the butter in a three-quart, heavy-bottomed saucepan until soft and transparent.

In a separate pan, melt the remaining butter, stir in the flour and cook, stirring, for one minute without browning. Gradually add the chicken stock. Stir until you have a thin sauce without any lumps. Pour this sauce over the onions, add the cider and the bouquet garni and simmer for fifteen minutes, stirring occasionally.

Just before serving, remove the bouquet garni, stir in the cream and pour into individual bowls. Place a few apple segments and some toasted croutons in each bowl, sprinkle with Gruyère cheese and place under a broiler for one minute.

6 SERVINGS

Turnip and Scallion Soup

Preparing soup for the indigent was a favorite philanthropic occupation of many a Victorian lady. Here is an updated version of a classic from that period and tradition. The addition of scallions (be sure to include the green part as well as the white) not only makes it look very pretty but provides an interesting contrasting crunchy texture that lifts this soup into the realm of the special.

4 medium-sized turnips, peeled and coarsely chopped
2 medium-sized potatoes, peeled and coarsely chopped
2 medium-sized onions, peeled and coarsely chopped

6 cups chicken stock
1 cup heavy cream
Salt
Freshly ground black pepper
Milk
1 bunch scallions, finely chopped

Place the turnips, potatoes and onions in a three-quart saucepan with the chicken stock. Bring to a boil and simmer for 30 minutes or until the vegetables are very soft.

Blend to a fine purée in a blender or by passing the soup through a sieve. Return the soup to a clean saucepan. Stir in the cream and season to taste with salt and pepper. If the soup seems too thick, add a little milk. Reheat but do not boil and pour into separate bowls. Scatter a generous amount of scallions on top of each portion.

6 SERVINGS

Mustard and Mushroom Soup

Here is a wonderful soup I came across recently in a small country pub in Sussex. Unfortunately the cook had vanished and no one was able to find her recipe before I had to leave so I have had to re-create it as best I can. Rich and satisfying, it's a soup to be served with hot, crusty bread.

4 *tablespoons unsalted butter*
2 *medium-sized onions,*
  finely chopped
¾ *pound mushrooms, sliced*
  in mushroom shapes
2 *cups heavy cream*
3 *cups milk*

3 *tablespoons Dijon mustard*
  or 1 teaspoon prepared
  English mustard
Juice of one lemon
Salt
Freshly ground black
pepper

Melt the butter in a large saucepan and add the onions. Cook for about three minutes or until the onions are soft but not brown. Add the mushrooms and cook over gentle heat for another three minutes. Add the cream, milk and mustard. Heat gently, but do not allow the soup to boil.

When the soup is hot, pour in the lemon juice slowly, stirring all the time—the mixture will curdle if you add it too quickly. (Should this happen, however, strain the liquid from the mushrooms and onions and pulse in a blender or food processor for ten seconds.)

Season to taste with salt and pepper and serve immediately.

6 SERVINGS

Curried Parsnip Soup

The poor parsnip has been dreadfully maligned. This was not always the case, however, and Mrs. Beeton in her *Book of Household Management*, published in 1861, even writes of a family that became quite delirious with excitement at eating parsnips. In medieval times, the parsnip root was believed to hold magical, healing powers. I, myself, have discovered, only rather late in life, how good parsnips can be, so I was delighted to be sent this recipe for a parsnip soup by Noreen Hope, who, as a member of At Home, frequently entertains American visitors at her home, Blunts Chase in Essex.

1 *pound parsnips*	4½ *cups chicken stock*
6 *tablespoons unsalted butter*	*Salt*
1 *large onion, finely chopped*	*Freshly ground black*
2 *cloves garlic, finely*	*pepper*
chopped	*Milk*
⅓ *cup flour*	2 *scallions, chopped*
2 *teaspoons Madras curry*	
powder	

Scrape and cut the parsnips into small pieces. Heat the butter in a three-quart saucepan. Add the parsnips, onion and garlic and sauté over gentle heat for five minutes. Stir in the flour and curry powder and gradually pour in the stock, stirring all the time. Bring to a boil and simmer for fifteen minutes or until the parsnips are tender.

Purée the mixture in a blender or food processor. Season to taste with salt and pepper and add a little milk if the consistency of the soup is too thick. Reheat gently and serve hot with scallions sprinkled on top.

4 TO 6 SERVINGS

Welsh Leek Soup

The leek is the national emblem of Wales and, not surprisingly, at the heart of many a Welsh dish. There are numerous recipes for leek soups; Mrs. Beeton's includes a sheep's head so I refrain from offering it. My own favorite contains no animal heads nor, interestingly, does it contain any potatoes, which tend to be found in most leek soups. In this recipe, the leeks are not puréed but still the soup is rich and smooth. The addition of a little Parmesan cheese enhances the flavor although I suspect that anyone Welsh would consider this a flagrant transgression.

5 *good-sized leeks*
4 *tablespoons unsalted butter*
4 *slices bacon*
2 *tablespoons flour*
4 *cups chicken stock*
1 *cup heavy cream*

¼ *cup chopped parsley*
2½ *tablespoons grated Parmesan cheese*
Salt
Freshly ground black pepper
Croutons

Wash, trim and slice the leeks into thin rounds, retaining some of the green leaves. Melt the butter in a large saucepan, chop the bacon into small pieces and place in the saucepan together with the leeks. Sauté for two minutes so that the leeks are thoroughly coated with the fat, then cover and cook over low heat for ten minutes.

Stir in the flour, cook for one minute and then pour in the stock. Bring to a boil while stirring all the time. Remove from the heat and stir in the cream, parsley and cheese. Check the seasoning and add salt and pepper to taste. Reheat briefly, if necessary, but do not boil. Serve with croutons.

4 TO 6 SERVINGS

Fish Soups

Curried Fish Soup

This soup can be served hot or chilled. I find that a luke-warm temperature is ideal.

1 *pound fillets of any*
white fish
4 *tablespoons unsalted*
butter
2 *tablespoons flour*
2¼ *cups chicken stock*
3 *teaspoons curry powder*
Juice of one lemon
3 *cups half-and-half*
Milk

Salt
Freshly ground black
pepper
1 *cup cooked, peeled*
shrimp, cut into pieces if
very large
10 *coriander leaves*
(cilantro), coarsely
chopped

Remove any skin and bones from the fish fillets. Melt the butter in a large saucepan and add the fish. Coat the fillets with the butter and then stir in the flour. Cook for one minute and then add the chicken stock gradually, stirring all the time.

Bring to a boil and add the curry powder. Simmer for ten minutes and add the lemon juice. Purée in a blender or food processor and return to a clean saucepan. Add the half-and-half and season to taste with salt and pepper. If the soup seems too thick, add a little milk.

Reheat the soup gently but do not allow to boil and just before serving add the shrimp and the coriander leaves.

4 SERVINGS

Smoked Haddock and Leek Soup

Cockie Leekie is a famous old Scottish soup made of chickens and prunes. Christopher Oakes, one of the new breed of talented young British chefs who presides over the kitchen of the Castle Hotel in Taunton, has invented his own version of this traditional classic by ingeniously adding smoked haddock to its chicken, prune and leek base.

2 *chickens (can be old and*	¾ *pound smoked haddock*
scraggy)	4 *pitted prunes*
4 *leeks*	*Salt*
6 *egg whites*	*Freshly ground black*
	pepper

Cut each chicken into four pieces and wash under cold water. Pat dry with a paper towel. Wash and trim three of the leeks and place them with the chicken in a four-quart saucepan. Cover with water (about eight to ten cups) and bring to a boil. Cover and simmer for three hours. Check from time to time and if necessary add more water to keep the chicken pieces covered with water.

Strain the stock into a clean saucepan and allow it to cool. Return to medium heat and beat in the egg whites to clear the stock. Bring the soup once more to a boil and simmer uncovered for another fifteen minutes until the stock has reduced to an amber color. Strain through a double thickness of fine cheesecloth.

Remove any skin and bones from the haddock and chop the flesh into small pieces. Wash the remaining leek and cut it and the prunes into julienne strips. Shortly before serving, reheat the soup and when it is hot add the haddock and leek strips, cook for one minute, add the prunes and season to taste with salt and pepper.

4 TO 6 SERVINGS

Note: For a more substantial soup, remove the skin from the chicken pieces and cut the meat into julienne strips. Add the chicken at the same time as the haddock.

Water Souchet

A delicious fish soup consisting of whole fillets of white fish served in a green, parsley-based stock. The name comes from Sootje and was originally a Dutch recipe introduced into England during the reign of William III. Serve the soup with lots of warm French bread. With cheese and a salad it will suffice for a meal.

1 *tablespoon vegetable oil*
1 *small onion, chopped*
2 *pounds non-oily fish bones*
    and fish heads
10 *peppercorns*
1 *teaspoon salt*

2 *cups white wine*
3 *large bunches parsley*
1 *pound flounder, cod or*
    scrod fillets
2 *lemons*

Heat the oil in a large saucepan, add the chopped onion and sauté over gentle heat until softened. Add the fish bones and fish heads, peppercorns, salt, white wine and four cups of water. Chop all the parsley including the stalks; reserve two tablespoons but add all the rest to the broth. Bring to a boil and simmer, half covered, for 40 minutes. Strain the stock and reserve all the liquid. This can all be done ahead of time. However, do not proceed with the rest of the recipe until ten minutes before serving.

Place the fish fillets in a wide, shallow, flameproof pan. Add enough of the fish stock to cover them and poach uncovered for five minutes so that they are just cooked but not overdone and flaky. Transfer the fish to heated soup bowls and quickly reheat the rest of the broth, adding the juice of one lemon. Pour the broth over the fish. Garnish with the remaining parsley and slices of the second lemon.

4 TO 6 SERVINGS

Mussel and Saffron Soup

Here's another soup that comes from Michael Quinn, formerly of the Ritz and now at Ettington Park. Since his recipe provides for twenty servings, I have reduced the quantities to a more manageable level. However, in all other respects, this *is* his soup.

2 *quarts mussels (about* 45
  mussels)
1 *large onion, finely*
  chopped
4 *tablespoons unsalted*
  butter
2½ *cups white wine*
1 *cup chopped celery*

3 *fresh or canned tomatoes,*
  peeled and chopped
½ *teaspoon saffron strands*
1 *cup heavy cream*
Salt
Freshly ground black
  pepper
Milk

Soak the mussels in salty water for 30 minutes and then scrub and beard them.

Sweat the onion in half the butter in a four-quart saucepan for five minutes, until soft and transparent. Add the mussels, the wine and two cups of water. Cover and bring to a boil. Boil for approximately five minutes, shaking the pan from time to time until the mussels have opened up. Remove the mussels, in their shells, from the liquid. When cool enough to handle, remove the mussels from their shells, pouring back into the pan any juice that accumulates, and set aside.

Sauté the celery in the remaining butter in a clean saucepan until it is soft. Add the mussel stock and boil until it is reduced by one-third. Add the tomatoes, all but twelve of the mussels and the saffron. Simmer gently for five minutes, then purée in a blender or food processor before returning the soup to a clean saucepan.

Add the cream and season to taste with salt and pepper. If the soup is too thick, add a little milk. Reheat to just below boiling, add the remaining mussels and serve.

4 TO 6 SERVINGS

Oyster and Guinness Soup

Wheelers, a group of London restaurants that specializes in seafood, serves this soup when oysters are in season. It is wonderful, and they very kindly let me have their recipe. I have adjusted their proportions slightly, as a little Guinness seems to go a longer way on this side of the Atlantic, but if you've a taste for it, add a bit more before serving. (Should oysters be unobtainable or too expensive, substitute the same number of clams or mussels.)

4 tablespoons unsalted butter
1 medium-sized onion, finely chopped
1/4 cup chopped celery
2 carrots, finely chopped
2 leeks, cleaned, trimmed and chopped
2 tablespoons flour
1 cup fish stock or 1/2 cup white wine and 1/2 cup water

1/2 cup Guinness
2 cups milk
2 egg yolks
1 cup heavy cream
15 raw oysters
Salt
Freshly ground black pepper
1/2 cup chopped parsley

Melt the butter in a saucepan over gentle heat. Add the onion and sauté it until it is soft. Add the celery, carrots and leeks and cook for five minutes.

Stir in the flour and gradually pour in the fish stock, Guinness and milk, stirring all the time. When the mixture is heated through, combine the egg yolks with the cream and add to the soup, together with the oysters. Simmer for two minutes but do not allow to boil or the eggs will curdle the soup. Season to taste with salt and pepper. Sprinkle with parsley before serving.

4 SERVINGS

Summer Soups

Chilled Gingered Carrot and Orange Soup

As anyone who watched *Upstairs Downstairs* knows, the BBC culinary consultant who was in charge of what went on in Mrs. Bridges's kitchen must have been someone to reckon with. He is Michael Smith, and has since then added all the food served on *The Duchess of Duke Street* to his credit. He is a food writer, journalist and lecturer, and has done a great deal to advance the cause of "good" English food. He is also the founder of the English House, a charming restaurant in Chelsea that specializes in contemporary editions of eighteenth- and nineteenth-century English dishes. Here is his contemporary version of a popular traditional soup. It is wonderfully bracing, especially on hot days.

1½ *pounds carrots*
2½ *cups chicken stock*
    Grated rind of one orange
  1 *teaspoon ground ginger*
  ½ *teaspoon mace*
1½ *cups orange juice*

2 *cups light cream*
    Salt
    Freshly ground black
    pepper
1 *cup sour cream*

Peel and cut the carrots into small slices. Simmer in the chicken stock, together with the orange rind, ginger and mace until tender. Set aside and allow to cool.

Blend to a fine purée in a food processor or blender. Stir in the orange juice and cream and season to taste with salt and pepper.

Chill for at least four hours. Serve with a dollop of sour cream in each serving.

6 SERVINGS

Pea, Lemon and Mint Soup

Imogen Skirving is another member of At Home, the organization started by Gretchen Stevens, an American who has lived for many years in England. Under the auspices of this program, foreign tourists can stay in a small number of private homes that have been specially selected to appeal to the most discriminating travelers. Only one party of guests is resident at any time so the hospitality is highly individual. Most of the houses in the plan are in the south of England; Langar Hall, the home of Mrs. Skirving, however, is in Nottinghamshire. She frequently serves this soup, which is an adaptation of an old English recipe, to her guests.

2 *medium-sized onions,*
  chopped
1 *lemon, cut into wedges*
  and seeds removed
1½ *pounds peas, fresh or*
  frozen
1 *handful fresh mint*

4 *cups chicken stock*
1 *cup heavy cream*
  Salt
  Freshly ground black
  pepper
  Cream or milk

Place the onions and the lemon in a saucepan; cover and sweat for fifteen minutes. Add the peas and all the mint except for a few small leaves and sweat for another ten minutes. Remove the lemon wedges after first squeezing them into the mixture.

Purée the pea mixture in a food processor or blender. If you want an extra-smooth soup you should also strain it through a sieve. Place the puréed soup in a saucepan, add the stock and bring it slowly to a boil.

Remove the soup from the heat and stir in the cream. Season to taste with salt and pepper. Add more cream or milk if you find the consistency too thick. The soup can be served hot or cold. Garnish before serving with the remaining mint leaves.

4 TO 6 SERVINGS

Cream of Celery and Stilton Soup

Michael's Nook is a small, luxurious country house hotel set in the hills about Grasmere in the Lake District. Visiting on an extremely hot summer's day, I was lucky enough to find this soup on the menu for lunch. The taste was both unusual and very refreshing. Having now made it several times myself, I am still surprised by how well the combination of celery and Stilton works, and how clever the two young chefs at Michael's Nook, Paul Vidic and Philip Vickery, were to think of putting them together.

2 medium-sized onions
1 medium-sized bunch celery, cleaned of all dirt
3 tablespoons unsalted butter
⅓ cup flour
3¾ cups chicken stock

1¼ cups heavy cream
½ pound Stilton cheese, grated
Salt
Freshly ground black pepper

Chop the onions and shred the celery. Melt the butter in a heavy-bottomed saucepan. Add the onions and celery and cook over gentle heat for approximately seven minutes. Stir in the flour and cook for another two minutes.

Add the stock slowly, stirring all the time, and bring to a boil. Carefully skim any impurities from the surface of the soup and simmer for 20 minutes.

Purée the soup in a blender or a food processor and strain through a fine sieve. Return the soup to a clean saucepan. Add the cream and the grated cheese and season to taste with salt and pepper. Serve lukewarm.

6 SERVINGS

Saffron and Leek Soup

Shaun Hill is one of the founding members of Country Chefs Seven, an organization of young British chefs who take their profession extremely seriously and have not a trace of a French accent among them. Formerly the chef at the Lygon Arms in the Cotswolds, Hill is now the owner and chef of Hill's at Stratford-upon-Avon. This recipe for leek soup, which, unlike my own, does contain potatoes, is frequently to be found on his menu.

5 to 6 leeks, cleaned and
    trimmed
3 medium-sized onions
2 celery stalks
6 medium-sized potatoes,
    peeled
6 cups chicken stock
    Bouquet garni (thyme, bay
    leaf and parsley)

½ teaspoon saffron strands
¼ teaspoon salt, or as needed
1 cup heavy cream
1 cup milk, or as needed
    Freshly ground black
    pepper
1 lemon, sliced

Cut all the vegetables into small cubes and place them in a large saucepan. Add the stock, herbs, saffron and ¼ teaspoon salt. Bring to a boil, cover and simmer until the vegetables are tender (about fifteen minutes). Purée in a blender or food processor and return to the saucepan. Stir in the cream and 1 cup milk; if the soup seems too thick add a little more milk. Season to taste with additional salt and pepper.

Serve hot or cold and place a slice of lemon on top of the soup in each bowl.

6 SERVINGS

Curried Apple Soup

An updated version of Mulligatawny soup—a hot, curry soup much favored by British colonials. This version is not only creamier and sweeter but has a far lighter texture.

4 *tablespoons unsalted butter*
3 *medium-sized onions, finely chopped*
3 *teaspoons curry powder*
1½ *tablespoons flour*
2 *cups country cider or unsweetened apple juice*
4 *cups chicken stock*
½ *cup heavy cream*
4 *egg yolks*

3 *teaspoons chopped parsley*
2 *teaspoons lemon juice*
2 *apples, peeled, cored and finely diced*
Salt
Freshly ground black pepper
1 *lemon, cut into six round slices*

Melt the butter in a large saucepan and add the onions. Cover and sweat the onions for approximately ten minutes. Add the curry powder and flour and cook for one minute while stirring. Gradually pour in the cider or juice and the stock, stirring all the while. Bring to a boil and simmer for two minutes before removing from the heat.

In a bowl, beat together the cream and egg yolks and whisk the mixture slowly into the soup. Return the saucepan to low heat and cook until the soup thickens to the consistency of heavy cream. Add the parsley, lemon juice and apples just before serving, and season to taste with salt and pepper. Decorate each bowl of soup with a slice of lemon.

The soup can also be served chilled. In that case, however, do not add the parsley and the apples until you are ready to serve the soup.

6 SERVINGS

First Courses

Here is a collection of first courses with many traditional ingredients appearing in some very nontraditional guises. A successful first course should stimulate the appetite and raise expectations for what is to come next. It can also inject a little surprise into the proceedings, and these recipes have been chosen with that, too, in mind.

Some savouries are also included in this chapter. Although few people still serve a separate savoury course, many of them make wonderful first courses. Being usually movable feasts, they also work well for lunch.

Many of these recipes call for individual ramekins but can of course be prepared in a single dish. I prefer to use ramekins as the results, especially for soufflés, are so much more attractive. I use ones that are approximately one and one-half inches high by three inches wide, but any medium-sized ramekin will do.

First Courses

Chicken Liver Parfait with
  Green Peppercorns
Port and Stilton Mousse
Stilton, Port and Celery
  Pâté
Deep-Fried Stilton Cheese
  Balls with Port Sauce
Seviche of Salmon
Potted Salmon

Smoked Haddock Mousse
  Wrapped in Spinach
Smoked Haddock in Puff
  Pastry
Smoked Haddock Soufflé
Watercress Pancakes
Sausage Rolls
Mrs. Gibson's Egg Dish
Eggs Madras

Savouries

Devils on Horseback
Kipper Rarebit
Kipper Savouries

Devilled Kidneys
Grilled Kidneys and
  Oysters

Chicken Liver Parfait
with Green Peppercorns

Gravetye Manor has long set the standard for the English country house hotel and is probably the best known. "How does it compare to Gravetye?" is a question I am frequently asked, and with good reason. For Gravetye is indeed exceptional—an elegant, sixteenth-century manor house set in the rolling parkland of West Sussex and surrounded by exquisite gardens laid out by William Robinson, the famous Edwardian landscape gardener who himself lived at Gravetye for over 50 years.

Peter Herbert, a jovial, energetic perfectionist, is responsible for creating the charm and comfort of Gravetye, and Allan Garth, a young, talented Englishman, is the head chef. The food at Gravetye is memorable and should not be missed. Many of the dishes are too complicated to be attempted by the nonprofessional, but this chicken liver pâté, made with port, Madeira and green peppercorns, is not difficult and should be tried.

Note that the chicken livers and the green peppercorns and raisins need to be marinated the night before you prepare the rest of this recipe.

½ *pound chicken livers,* *cleaned*	8 *tablespoons unsalted* *butter*
About 1 *cup milk*	1 *pound fresh pork fat, cut* *into thin slices*
12 *green peppercorns*	
¼ *cup golden seedless raisins*	Salt
1 *tablespoon Madeira*	*Freshly ground black* *pepper*
1 *tablespoon port*	1 *sprig fresh thyme*

The night before preparing the parfait, place the chicken livers in a glass or porcelain bowl and pour in just enough milk to cover. Place in the refrigerator. Marinate the peppercorns and raisins in the Madeira and port at room temperature.

Clarify the butter by melting in a small saucepan without browning. Skim any foam off the top and spoon out the now clear or "clarified" butter.

Line a medium-sized terrine with the slices of pork fat. Strain and discard the milk from the chicken livers and place them in a food processor. Pulse and slowly add the warm, clarified butter. Stir in the peppercorns and raisins and their marinade. Season with salt and pepper and spoon the mixture into the terrine. Place a sprig of thyme on top and cover with more slices of pork fat.

Preheat the oven to 250°.

Wrap the top of the terrine with a layer of foil, cover and place the terrine in a pan of boiling water. The water should come about halfway up the outside of the terrine. Cook in the oven for one hour and then test to see if the pâté is ready: press the top, the pâté is done if it is firm and it has shrunk slightly from the sides of the dish.

Allow the pâté to cool at room temperature for several hours and serve with toast.

1 MEDIUM-SIZED LOAF OR 2 CUPS

Port and Stilton Mousse

Murdo MacSween is a Hebridean shepherd's son with an engaging enthusiasm for all things gastronomic. He is also one of the founding members of Country Chefs Seven—the group of chefs who formed an organization to dramatize the fact that there are some young British chefs who take their profession seriously—and is in charge of the kitchen at the Oakley Court Hotel near Windsor. This recipe is an excellent example of contemporary British inventiveness: traditional ingredients brought together to make a new and original dish. In making this dish, use white port if at all possible as the red gives the mousse a rather unattractive, indeterminate pink cast. Serve with toast or crackers.

½ pound Stilton cheese, grated
½ cup white port
1 cup heavy cream
4 egg whites
½ cup crushed walnuts

1 packet unflavored gelatin
Salt
Freshly ground black pepper
2 tablespoons finely chopped chives

Blend together the Stilton, port and cream. Beat the egg whites until stiff and fold into the mixture together with the crushed walnuts.

Dissolve the gelatin in a little hot water and stir into the mixture. Season to taste with salt and pepper and pour into six individual ramekins.

Refrigerate for at least two hours. Ten minutes before serving, remove the ramekins from the refrigerator and sprinkle with the chives.

6 SERVINGS

Stilton, Port and Celery Pâté

Stilton and port traditionally belong at the end of a meal. This recipe, given to me by Sam Chalmers of Le Talbooth in Dedham near Colchester, offers a way to move them up to the beginning. In addition to making a good first course, this pâté can be served with crackers for an hors d'oeuvre.

3 tablespoons unsalted butter
6 tablespoons flour
2 cups milk
½ stalk celery, finely
chopped
1 clove garlic, crushed
¼ cup port
10 pitted imported Italian
olives

½ cup heavy cream
¼ cup mayonnaise
½ pound Stilton cheese,
grated
Salt
Freshly ground black
pepper
Hot toast

Melt the butter in a saucepan over gentle heat. Stir in the flour and cook together for a minute. Gradually add the milk, stirring constantly. Bring the sauce just to a boil, then simmer for ten minutes, continuing to stir. Allow to cool.

Mix the cooled sauce with the celery, garlic, port, olives, cream and mayonnaise. When all the ingredients are thoroughly mixed, fold in the Stilton. Season to taste with salt and pepper. Pour into ramekins, refrigerate until ten minutes before serving, and serve with hot toast.

6 SERVINGS OR 2 CUPS

Deep-Fried Stilton Cheese Balls
with Port Sauce

¾ pound Stilton cheese
2 egg yolks
¼ teaspoon paprika
2 eggs, beaten with a little
   water
2 cups fresh breadcrumbs
Oil for deep frying

SAUCE

¾ cup port
½ cup red currant jelly
   Juice of one orange
   Juice of one lemon
2 teaspoons arrowroot

Crumble the Stilton and mix it together with the egg yolks and the paprika. Form the mixture into little balls (approximately one inch in diameter); dip each ball into the egg and water mixture, then roll in the breadcrumbs. Chill in the refrigerator for 30 minutes.

To make the sauce: Combine the port, red currant jelly, orange and lemon juices in a small saucepan. Bring to a boil. Place the arrowroot in a cup and pour over a little of the liquid to dissolve it. Return to the saucepan. Continue to stir until the sauce has thickened. Set aside.

In a deep fryer, fry the Stilton balls until they are golden. Transfer them to plates, reheat the sauce if necessary and serve on the side.

4 TO 6 SERVINGS

Seviche of Salmon

So often the most memorable dishes are the simplest to prepare. This recipe, which I had on a recent visit to Sharrow Bay, is a case in point. Sharrow Bay is a hotel magically situated on the edge of Lake Ullswater in the Lake District. It is filled with overstuffed chairs, fresh flowers and objets d'art, and visitors are offered amazing hospitality and comfort. As the food is often extremely rich, this recipe in some ways is not typical of most Sharrow Bay fare. Nevertheless, it proved the ideal beginning for a six-course dinner I had there one night.

1 *pound salmon fillets, cut into small strips*
½ *cup dry white wine*
½ *cup walnut or sunflower oil*
1 *shallot, diced*
1 *clove garlic, crushed*

Juice and grated peel of one lemon
Juice and grated peel of one orange
1½ *teaspoons salt*
Dill

Mix all the ingredients but the dill in a bowl. Cover and refrigerate for ten to twelve hours. Sprinkle some dill over the salmon before serving on individual plates.

6 SERVINGS

Potted Salmon

Potting was, traditionally, in the days before refrigeration, an excellent way of preserving food over a considerable period of time. Potted fish and meat have always been popular in Britain. Less familiar than potted shrimps, but equally delicious, is potted salmon. This dish originally came from Newcastle, a major port close to salmon fishing waters and once the main transit point for Scotch salmon heading to London.

¾ pound salmon fillets
8 tablespoons unsalted
*   butter, cut into small*
*   slices*
½ teaspoon mace
¼ teaspoon ground ginger
1 tablespoon chopped
*   parsley*

½ teaspoon salt
½ teaspoon ground white
*   pepper*
1 tablespoon lemon juice
1½ cups medium-dry sherry
6 tablespoons unsalted
*   butter (for clarified*
*   butter)*

Preheat the oven to 325°.

Place the salmon in a small ovenproof dish. Dot it with the butter and sprinkle with the mace, ginger, parsley, salt and pepper. Combine the lemon juice and sherry and pour over the fish. Cut a piece of waxed paper the size of the dish and place it over the fish. Cover the dish with a tight-fitting lid or a piece of foil.

Cook in the preheated oven for one hour. Uncover and let the fish cool to room temperature; remove the lid and waxed paper. Lift out the fish with a slotted spatula. Reserve the cooking juices in the pan. Remove any skin from the salmon and pull out any small bones (a tweezer can be useful here).

Cut the salmon into diagonal slices and divide into four portions. Place each portion into an individual ramekin.

Strain the cooking juices into a small saucepan and boil rapidly until reduced to one-third of a cup. Divide equally over the salmon. Cover each ramekin with a piece of foil and weigh down with a small can. Refrigerate for at least one hour, then remove the weight and uncover the salmon.

To prepare the clarified butter: Melt the butter in a small saucepan, skim any foam off the top and spoon out the clear—"clarified"—butter. Pour it over the ramekins, dividing evenly to cover the tops. Cover and refrigerate. Serve cold.

Potted salmon can be stored in the refrigerator for at least a week.

4 SERVINGS

Smoked Haddock Mousse Wrapped in Spinach

This is my attempt to re-create a dish I have often enjoyed in England. It is important to use only fresh spinach in this recipe as the individual leaves cannot be separated satisfactorily once the spinach has been frozen.

1 *pound fresh spinach*	2 *egg yolks*
¾ *pound smoked haddock*	*Juice of half a lemon*
Freshly ground black	¼ *cup heavy cream*
pepper	*Salt*
2 *tablespoons unsalted butter*	2 *egg whites*
½ *cup milk*	1 *cucumber, thinly sliced*
1 *packet unflavored gelatin*	

Preheat oven to 400°.

Wash the spinach and remove the stalks. Plunge the leaves into a saucepan that contains a small amount of boiling water. Stir for ten seconds or just enough time for the leaves to go limp. Drain well on paper towels.

Place the haddock in a baking dish. Sprinkle with a little pepper and dot with the butter. Partially cover with the milk and a little boiling water. Cover and cook in the oven until the fish is cooked (approximately ten minutes).

Remove and discard any bones from the fish and place it in a food processor. Dissolve the gelatin in two tablespoons of boiling water and add it to the fish, together with the egg yolks. Process for half a minute and then add the lemon juice and cream. Process again briefly and then season to taste with salt and pepper. Beat the egg whites until stiff and then fold them into the fish mixture.

Grease eight ramekins and line them with the spinach leaves, leaving a large part of the leaves hanging over the edge. Place some of the fish mixture in each ramekin and fold over the spinach leaves so as to cover the fish completely. Refrigerate for at least four hours.

To serve, remove the ramekins from the refrigerator fifteen minutes before serving. Turn them upside down on separate plates and gently shake out the fish packages. Arrange the cucumber slices around the fish and serve.

8 SERVINGS

Smoked Haddock in Puff Pastry

Smoked haddock with chives and cream baked in puff pastry cases makes a delectable first course. Here it is, as served at Milton Sandford, an excellent restaurant at Shinfield, near Reading.

6 *ounces Puff Pastry (see next recipe) or 4 vol-au-vent cases*
1 *egg mixed with about 1 tablespoon milk*
¾ *pound smoked haddock*

1 *cup milk*
4 *tablespoons unsalted butter*
1 *cup chopped mushrooms*
1 *shallot, finely chopped*
2 *teaspoons chopped chives*
⅓ *cup heavy cream*

Preheat the oven to 350°.

Roll out the pastry to a thickness of approximately one-eighth of an inch. Using a biscuit or cookie cutter, cut into rounds approximately four inches in diameter. With a small cutter or glass, lightly press a circle about two inches in diameter in the middle of each round of pastry. Brush the pastry cases with the egg and milk mixture, place them on a cookie sheet and bake until the pastry is golden brown (about 20 minutes). If using frozen vol-au-vent cases follow the cooking directions on the package.

While the pastry is cooking, place the haddock in a shallow pan with the milk and one cup of water and poach for five minutes or until the haddock can be easily flaked into pieces. Discard the cooking liquid and set the fish aside.

In a clean saucepan, melt the butter and sauté the chopped mushrooms, shallot and chives. When they are soft, add the flaked haddock and the cream. Bring slowly to a simmer and remove from heat.

When the pastry cases have cooled slightly, cut off their tops and scoop out any soggy pastry from the inner circle. Gently reheat the haddock mixture if necessary, place inside the pastry cases, replace the lids and serve.

4 SERVINGS

Puff Pastry

This recipe makes a little over twelve ounces of puff pastry, which is the right amount for almost all the recipes in this book which call for puff pastry. For the others—Smoked Haddock in Puff Pastry, Apple Tart with Calvados, Brown Sugar and Tarragon, and any other recipes that call for six ounces of puff pastry—use half the quantities given here. However, since puff pastry freezes very well and it is difficult to make in small quantities, I would recommend making the amount given in this recipe, or even double this amount, and freezing what you don't use. Be sure to completely wrap the pastry that is to be frozen, and allow it to defrost slowly in the refrigerator for 24 hours before using.

2 *cups unbleached flour*	½ *pound unsalted butter*
1 *teaspoon salt*	About ½ *cup ice water*

Sift the flour and the salt into a large bowl. Cut four tablespoons of the butter into small pieces and work them into the flour with your fingers until the mixture resembles coarse breadcrumbs. Add enough ice water to turn the mixture into a stiff dough. Work the dough quickly into a ball, dust lightly with flour and place in a plastic bag. Refrigerate for at least one hour.

Using your fingers, soften the remaining butter and work it into a square about four inches across. Place this square between two sheets of waxed paper and roll it smooth. Remove the top sheet of waxed paper and sprinkle the butter with a little flour. Wrap in fresh paper and refrigerate until the butter is firm.

Take the dough and butter from the refrigerator and remove the waxed paper.

Roll out the dough into a square approximately twelve inches by twelve inches. Place the butter diagonally in the center. Bring the corners of the dough over the butter to make a closure similar to an envelope.

Dust the dough package with a little flour and roll into a rectangle approximately six inches by ten inches, the long sides running top to bottom. Fold the top of the dough over all but the bottom third of the rectangle. Now fold the bottom third over the top and turn the dough so that one of the open ends is facing you.

Roll the dough from the center to the edge furthest away from you, stopping before the very edge so as not to let the butter come out. Turn the pastry around and roll the other half out and away from you until you have a rectangle about twelve inches long. Fold the dough into thirds as before. Wrap it in waxed paper and chill in the refrigerator for 30 minutes.

Remove the dough from the refrigerator, take off the paper, flour the board and the dough and roll the dough out exactly as before, always away from you. Fold it into thirds again and repeat the rolling out process. Chill the dough for at least another 30 minutes. It is now ready to be used. The dough can be refrigerated for four to five days or it can be frozen for several months, if first wrapped in plastic and then in foil.

12 OUNCES

Smoked Haddock Soufflé

In Britain, smoked haddock is a comforting, if somewhat plebeian, fish that used to be served most often in kedgeree or finnan haddie. However, its golden color and distinctive smokey flavor offer a rich field for culinary experimentation and in the past few years it has begun to appear under many different guises. This recipe makes an excellent first course. Trial and much error have convinced me that it is best to serve this or, for that matter, any soufflé in individual ramekins, since it is something that never looks its best once it has been served onto a plate, where it inevitably collapses.

The soufflé base and the sauce can be made several hours in advance.

½ *pound smoked haddock*	*Salt*
1 *cup milk*	*Nutmeg*
6 *tablespoons unsalted*	
butter	SAUCE
Freshly ground black	
pepper	2 *egg yolks*
4 *tablespoons flour*	½ *cup heavy cream*
2 *cups light cream*	*Fish liquor from the above*
5 *egg yolks*	*recipe*
5 *egg whites*	¼ *cup chopped parsley*

Place the haddock in a shallow pan and cover with the milk. Dot one tablespoon of the butter on top of the haddock, season with pepper and bring the milk to the boiling point. Cover and simmer gently until the haddock is tender, about ten minutes. Strain the cooking liquid and set aside. Flake the fish into small pieces using a fork, and remove any skin or bones.

Melt the remaining butter in a saucepan, add the flour and cook gently for three minutes. Pour in the cream slowly, stirring all the time. Bring very gradually to a boil and stir for one minute. Remove the sauce from the heat and allow to cool slightly, then beat in the egg yolks one at a time. Stir in the fish and season to taste with salt, pepper and nutmeg.

The next part of the recipe should not be completed until just before you wish to serve the soufflé.

Preheat the oven to 400°.

Beat the egg whites with a pinch of salt until they are stiff and fold them into the haddock mixture. Spoon this mixture into six well-greased ramekins. Cook in the preheated oven for ten to twelve minutes or until golden brown on top with the inside still creamy. Take care not to overcook.

To prepare the sauce: Beat the egg yolks, cream and the strained fish-cooking liquor in a double boiler set over simmering water until the sauce thickens. Before serving the soufflés, reheat the sauce if necessary. Cut a little notch in the top of each soufflé, dribble in a bit of the sauce and sprinkle some parsley on top.

6 SERVINGS

Watercress Pancakes

From Homewood Park, a rambling, beautifully furnished country house hotel just outside Bath that serves marvelous food, comes this very simple recipe for pancakes which are really sophisticated green crêpes. Anthony Pitt, the chef at Homewood, suggests using a creamed smoked haddock filling. However, any one of a number of savoury fillings work beautifully—try the Talbooth Soufflé (see page 80)—and for leftover chicken these pancakes are a godsend.

WATERCRESS PURÉE

1 *small onion, finely chopped*
2 *tablespoons unsalted butter*
½ *cup heavy cream, or more*
¼ *cup milk*
2 *bunches watercress (leaves only)*

PANCAKES

4 *tablespoons flour*
4 *eggs*
4 *tablespoons melted unsalted butter, cooled*
3 *tablespoons watercress purée*
Vegetable oil

To make the purée: Cover and sweat the onion in the butter over gentle heat in a heavy bottomed saucepan for about five minutes. Add the *half cup* cream and milk and bring slowly to a boil. Add the watercress leaves and cook for two minutes, stirring all the time. Remove from the heat and liquidize in a blender or food processor.

To make the pancakes: Combine the flour, eggs, melted butter and the watercress purée. Blend in a food processor or beat by hand until bubbles rise to the surface. Transfer the batter to a pitcher and allow to stand for at least 30 minutes.

Pour a little vegetable oil in a frying pan or crêpe pan approximately seven inches in diameter. Place over medium heat and tilt the pan until the oil covers the surface evenly. As soon as the oil begins to smoke, pour a little batter (about one-third of a cup) into the pan and turn the pan until the batter covers the surface. Turn the pancake when the underside is golden (about one minute) and cook on the other side for another two minutes. Slide the pancake onto a plate. Fill with a savoury filling, roll up the pancake and keep warm in the oven while making the rest of the pancakes in the same manner.

Use the remaining watercress purée as a sauce for the finished dish. If it seems a little too thick, dilute it with some additional cream.

4 TO 6 SERVINGS

Sausage Rolls

It's rare to find homemade sausage rolls today and the commercial variety found in many pubs has given them a deservedly dreadful reputation. But, sausage rolls come from a noble tradition of meat pies and, when homemade, they are most gratifying. Serve them as an hors d'oeuvre, as a first course or for brunch accompanied with Mustard and Dill Sauce (see page 148).

12 ounces Puff Pastry (see page 46)
¾ pound sausage meat
1 small onion, finely chopped
1 teaspoon sage
1 teaspoon thyme
1 teaspoon ground coriander or 2 tablespoons chopped fresh coriander (cilantro)
Salt
Freshly ground black pepper
1 egg yolk, beaten with a little water

Divide the pastry into four pieces and roll out into four rectangular shapes that measure approximately four by twelve inches each. Set aside.

Combine the sausage meat, onion and herbs in a mixing bowl. Add a generous amount of salt and pepper. Divide the mixture into four pieces and, using floured hands, shape each part into a twelve-inch roll. Place each roll on one of the pastry strips. Brush some of the egg yolk and water on one of the long pastry edges. Bring one side over to meet the other and press it down so that it is well sealed. Crimp the edges with a fork and cut each roll into three-inch lengths.

Preheat the oven to 400°.

Transfer the sausage rolls to a baking dish. Brush the tops with the remaining egg and water and make two slashes across the top of each roll in order to allow the steam to escape. Cook for 25 minutes or until the pastry is golden and crisp. Serve warm.

16 SAUSAGE ROLLS

Note: For cocktail hors d'oeuvres, cut the rolls into two-inch rather than three-inch lengths.

Mrs. Gibson's Egg Dish

This recipe was given to me by Ron Titley, former chef to the Marquis of Salisbury. Mrs. Gibson was a neighbor and friend of Lady Salisbury's and this was originally her recipe. Until recently, Ron Titley owned and ran his own restaurant, The Old Cottage, in King's Hagley, Hertfordshire.

1 *bunch scallions, finely chopped*	*Salt*
6 *tablespoons unsalted butter*	*Freshly ground black pepper*
6 *hard-boiled eggs*	1 *cup toasted breadcrumbs*
1¼ *cups heavy cream*	2 *tablespoons chopped parsley*

Preheat oven to 350°.

Sauté the scallions in the butter in a heavy saucepan. Coarsely chop the hard-boiled eggs, add them to the scallions and heat through for five minutes.

Place the mixture in a well-greased ovenproof dish or in separate ramekins and pour the cream over. Sprinkle with salt and pepper and cover with breadcrumbs.

Bake in the oven for ten minutes or until the dish is bubbling and brown.

Sprinkle with parsley and serve hot.

4 TO 6 SERVINGS

Eggs Madras

Mrs. Gibson's Egg Dish (see previous recipe) was so popular with customers at The Old Cottage that Ron Titley came up with his own variation on it, which proved equally popular. Both these recipes make excellent lunch dishes.

1 *small onion, finely chopped*
8 *tablespoons unsalted butter*
1 *tablespoon tomato paste*
2 *tablespoons mango chutney*
1 *heaping tablespoon Madras*
 curry powder
1 *cup heavy cream*

6 *hard-boiled eggs*
1 *cup toasted breadcrumbs*
Salt
Freshly ground black
pepper
2 *tablespoons chopped*
 parsley

Preheat oven to 350°.

Sauté the onion in four tablespoons of the butter in a heavy saucepan until it is soft. Add the tomato paste, chutney and curry powder. Stir over moderate heat for half a minute. Add the cream and gently simmer for another minute.

Chop the hard-boiled eggs and place them in an ovenproof dish or in separate ramekins. Pour the Madras sauce over and cover with the breadcrumbs. Dot the remaining butter on top and sprinkle with salt and pepper. Bake in the oven for approximately ten minutes until the dish is bubbling and brown.

Sprinkle with the parsley and serve.

4 TO 6 SERVINGS

Savouries

The following recipes are all savouries—a uniquely British culinary invention. Originally the word was used to distinguish a dish from one that was sweet (i.e., a sweetmeat), and in the seventeenth century a savoury might have been served at either the beginning or the end of a meal. However, by the nineteenth century, the savoury was firmly established as the last course and was considered to be useful as a digestive aid.

Savouries are rarely served as such today. But they have made a happy transition and prove exactly right for first courses or light lunch or brunch dishes.

Devils on Horseback

A favorite savoury with Victorians that has never gone out of fashion, these "devils" are a kind of opposite number to angels on horseback (chutneyed prunes rather than oysters wrapped in bacon) with a devilish involvement of hot English mustard. They make delicious hors d'oeuvres.

3 tablespoons hot chutney
2 teaspoons sliced almonds
16 pitted prunes
8 slices bacon, cut in half
4 tablespoons unsalted butter
¼ cup heavy cream

1½ tablespoons prepared
    English mustard

HOT BUTTERED TOAST

4 slices firm white bread
Unsalted butter

Mix together the chutney and almonds and stuff each prune with a little of the mixture. Wrap each prune with half a slice of bacon and secure with a toothpick.

Melt the butter in a frying pan and fry the prunes over medium heat until the bacon is crisp. Drain on paper towels.

Beat the cream until it is stiff and mix it with the mustard.

To make hot buttered toast: Preheat the oven to 400°. Trim the crusts off the slices of bread. Melt some butter and spread it on both sides of the bread. Place the buttered bread on a cookie sheet and place in the preheated oven for five minutes or until it is lightly browned on the bottom. Turn over and continue to cook for another two minutes until the new underside is also golden brown. Cut each slice into four squares. (If the recipe calls for triangles of toast, cut each square into two triangles.)

Serve each devil on a small square of hot toast, with a dollop of the mustard cream on either side.

16 DEVILS

Kipper Rarebit

Rarebit or rabbit—this controversy goes back to the eighteenth century. Does rarebit mean something sought after and underdone, or is it a corruption of rabbit, cheese being the poor man's substitute for meat? The arguments are murky on both sides and often seem to have more to do with politics than etymology.

The best known of the rabbits or rarebits is, of course, Welsh rarebit; but Kipper Rarebit is a new and interesting variation.

2 kippers	1/3 cup flour
1½ cups milk	1¼ cups grated Cheddar
2 cloves garlic, finely	cheese
chopped	1/8 teaspoon paprika
4 tablespoons unsalted	6 slices hot buttered toast
butter	(see previous recipe)

Place the kippers in a shallow pan with the milk. Bring to a boil and remove from the heat. Allow the kippers to steep in the milk for five minutes then lift out and remove the skin and bones. Return the filleted kipper to the milk, add the garlic and simmer for a further ten minutes. Strain, reserving the liquid.

Flake the kippers into small pieces. Melt the butter in a medium-sized saucepan. Stir in the flour and gradually pour in the reserved milk. Bring to a boil, stirring constantly. Fold in the grated cheese and the flaked kippers. Add the paprika for color. Heat thoroughly and pile on to the hot buttered toast. Serve immediately.

6 SERVINGS

Kipper Savouries

Another recipe for kipper aficionados.

2 *cooked kippers* (8 *fillets*)	*Freshly ground black*
2 *tablespoons heavy cream*	*pepper*
2 *hard-boiled eggs*	6 *slices hot buttered toast*
Juice of half a lemon	(*see page 56*)
Salt	6 *twists of cucumber*

Remove the skin and any bones from the kippers and flake into small pieces. Mix with the cream. Chop the eggs coarsely and add to the kipper mixture. Season to taste with the lemon, salt and pepper. Pile the mixture on to the slices of toast and place under a broiler for about three minutes to heat through. Decorate each portion with a twist of cucumber. Serve immediately.

6 SERVINGS

Devilled Kidneys

In addition to being served as a savoury Devilled Kidneys have always been popular as a breakfast dish. I also find they are an unfailing success if presented with Bloody Marys at a brunch.

2 *eggs*
2 *tablespoons prepared English mustard*
½ *teaspoon Worcestershire sauce*
½ *teaspoon Tabasco sauce*
Salt

8 *lamb or veal kidneys, skinned and diced*
1½ *cups fresh breadcrumbs*
6 *tablespoons unsalted butter*
12 *triangles hot buttered toast (see page 56)*

Beat the eggs and mix with the mustard, Worcestershire sauce, Tabasco and a pinch of salt. Coat the kidneys in the sauce and then roll them in the breadcrumbs.

Place the kidneys on skewers (this is optional, but it does prevent them from curling). Heat the butter in a frying pan large enough to fit the skewers and sauté the kidneys over medium heat for five to seven minutes, turning frequently— take care not to overcook.

Remove the kidneys from the skewers and serve with triangles of hot buttered toast.

6 SERVINGS

Grilled Kidneys and Oysters

Kidneys and oysters seem like a strange combination but they work wonderfully together; the notion of combining oysters with meat was in fact very common in the nineteenth century when oysters were extremely plentiful and cheap.

15 *oysters*
  Juice of half a lemon
  8 *lamb* or *veal kidneys,*
    skinned and diced
1½ *tablespoons flour*
  2 *tablespoons prepared*
    English mustard

  Salt
  4 *tablespoons unsalted*
    butter
  1 *teaspoon Worcestershire*
    sauce
12 *triangles hot buttered*
    toast (see page 56)

Remove the oysters from their shells and sprinkle with lemon juice. Dust the kidneys and the oysters with flour and roll them in the mustard. Sprinkle with a little salt and thread them on skewers, alternating oysters with kidneys. (The skewers are not essential but they do prevent the kidneys from curling.)

Melt the butter in a frying pan large enough to fit the skewers and fry the kidneys and the oysters for five to seven minutes, turning them frequently—take care not to overcook. While cooking, sprinkle them with the Worcestershire sauce.

Remove the kidneys and oysters from the skewers and serve with the triangles of hot buttered toast.

6 SERVINGS

Fish

Fish has always been plentiful in the British Isles and in
Victorian times each region of the country boasted its own
local fish. Even oysters, crabs and lobsters were all common,
everyday foods. In this century, fish has suffered at the
freezer's hands and the big processors have put many fish-
mongers out of business. As a result, it is much harder to
find good local fish today.

Smoked fish of course survives without freezing and has
remained a standby. In recent years, many British chefs and
cooks have experimented and come up with wonderfully
imaginative recipes for various smoked fish, in particular
haddock, some of which are included here. Another area for
innovation has been the traditional fish pie, which probably
originated as an economical way to feed a large family. It
is now making a successful comeback and interesting variations abound.

Fish

Salmon in Pastry with
    Ginger and Currants
Salmon in Pastry with
    Vermouth, Dill and
    Cream Sauce
Salmon and Dill Fishcakes
Salmon Kedgeree
Brandade of Smoked
    Mackerel
Trout Poached in Lemon
    and Thyme Stock
Scallop Mousse with
    Prawn Sauce

Scallop Salad
Scallops with Avocado
    Sauce
Lobster and Scallop Pie
Mussel and Onion Stew
Fish Pudding
Fish Choucroute
Smoked Haddock and
    Parsley Pie
Talbooth Soufflé

Salmon in Pastry with Ginger and Currants

The Carved Angel in Dartmouth is another restaurant that should be on all itineraries heading from London to the South-West of England. Joyce Molyneux is the guiding spirit behind this delightful restaurant on Dartmouth's waterfront. She specializes in local fish and this recipe, which is an adaptation of one from the seventeenth century, found in *The Good Housewife's Jewell* by Thomas Dawson, is one of her best. Serve it with Herb and Cream Sauce (see page 145).

1½–2 pounds salmon fillet
Salt
Freshly ground black
pepper
2 or 3 pieces preserved ginger
1 tablespoon currants

4 tablespoons unsalted
butter, softened
12 ounces Shortcrust
Pastry (see next recipe)
1 egg, beaten with about
1 tablespoon milk

Remove any skin from the fish and cut away any internal bones. Divide the fish into two horizontal slices and season with a little salt and pepper.

Rinse the ginger of its syrup. Chop finely and mix with the currants and butter. Spread the mixture over both slices of salmon and then make a sandwich of the two pieces.

Preheat oven to 400°.

Roll out the pastry, place the salmon in the middle and bring both ends of the pastry over to make a neat parcel. Trim the pastry and brush it with the egg and milk.

Place the salmon package in a well-greased baking dish and bake in the oven for 20 minutes. Reduce the temperature to 300° and bake for another ten to fifteen minutes, until golden.

4 TO 6 SERVINGS

Shortcrust Pastry

This recipe makes enough pastry (six ounces) to line or cover up to a nine-inch pan. For recipes that require twelve ounces of pastry, double the quantities given here.

1⅔ cups flour
  Pinch of salt
  8 tablespoons unsalted
    butter, cut into small
    pieces

2 teaspoons confectioners'
  sugar
1 egg yolk
2 teaspoons vegetable oil

Sift the flour and the salt into a bowl. Cut in the butter until the mixture resembles fine breadcrumbs. Stir in the confectioners' sugar and make a well in the center. Combine the egg yolk, oil and one and one-half tablespoons of cold water and pour into the well. Mix quickly with a fork and use your hands to press the dough into a ball. Wrap in waxed paper and refrigerate for at least 20 minutes before using.

6 OUNCES

Salmon in Pastry with Vermouth, Dill and Cream Sauce

The Peat Inn, near Fife on the east coast of Scotland, is the kind of place that occasionally gets recommended by people in the know—*occasionally* because they don't want *too* many others to know, after all. As the major guides put it, this restaurant is worth a detour for its excellent cooking with local ingredients and home-grown herbs. David and Patricia

Wilson, the chef-proprietors, serve the following dish, made of course with local salmon, together with a salmon mousse. My adaptation of their recipe omits the mousse as the combination is a trifle ambitious for the domestic cook.

12 *ounces Puff Pastry (see*
   page 46)
6 *six-ounce slices of salmon,*
   cut from one side of a
   salmon fillet and with the
   skin removed
Salt
Freshly ground black
pepper
1 *egg yolk, beaten with a*
   little water

SAUCE

⅔ *cup fish stock*
¼ *cup dry vermouth*
⅔ *cup heavy cream*
8 *tablespoons unsalted butter*
1 *teaspoon chopped dill*

Roll out the pastry on a cool surface until it is thin and almost transparent. It should be no thicker than fine writing paper. Place one portion of salmon on top of the pastry and sprinkle with a little salt and pepper. Cut the pastry around the salmon, leaving enough to fold over and meet in the center of the salmon with no overlap. Turn over and press down the sides. Score the top very lightly, making sure not to cut through the pastry, and refrigerate until ready to cook. Repeat with the other portions of salmon.

Preheat the oven to 450°.

Place the salmon packets on a cookie sheet. Brush with the egg yolk and water and cook in the oven for ten minutes or until the pastry is just golden. Do not overcook as it is important that the salmon be moist.

To prepare the sauce, which can be made in advance: Bring the stock to a boil in a saucepan. Add the vermouth and reduce to approximately one-half of a cup. Add the cream and then beat in the butter in small pieces. Season to taste and keep in a warm spot, but do not attempt to reheat. Add the dill just before serving.

To serve, place a separate portion of salmon on each plate and surround with a little sauce.

6 SERVINGS

Salmon and Dill Fishcakes

Fishcakes and tomato soup seem to share the same unhappy fate; they are rarely made fresh and their canned or frozen representatives simply cannot compare to the real thing. Few people know how delicious homemade fishcakes can be. Change their minds with this recipe that was given to me by Anthony Pitt of Homewood Park and serve the fishcakes with his Cucumber Sauce (see page 146). Together with soup and a salad, this makes a perfect pre- or post-theater dinner.

1 *pound salmon, cooked, with bones and skin removed*
2 *cups mashed potatoes, at room temperature*
2 *eggs*
1 *tablespoon chopped parsley*
1 *tablespoon chopped dill*

Nutmeg
Salt
Freshly ground black pepper
1 *cup breadcrumbs*
4 *tablespoons unsalted butter*

Blend together the salmon, potatoes, eggs, parsley and dill. Add a pinch of nutmeg and season generously with salt and pepper. Form into cakes about two and one-half inches in diameter (since the mixture will be rather sticky, dip your fingers into flour first) and roll each cake in the breadcrumbs. Refrigerate for at least 30 minutes.

Shortly before serving, fry the fishcakes gently in butter until they are crisp and golden on the outside.

4 SERVINGS

Salmon Kedgeree

Kedgeree was first brought to England by empire builders returning from the East. Its name comes from the Hindi *khichri*, an Indian dish made of split pulses (peas, beans, lentils, etc.), rice, onions, eggs and condiments. Apparently it was the English who first added any cold fish left over from the night before, and thereby created a combination so perfect that it was soon famous as "a capital thing to breakfast on." I had always assumed that kedgeree should be made with smoked haddock. However, Mrs. Beeton, the foremost authority on the eating habits of the Victorian middle classes, tells her readers simply to use "any cold [by which she means cooked] fish." Salmon elevates kedgeree to a new level of sophistication in both taste and color.

1 *pound salmon, any cut*
Salt
Freshly ground black
pepper
1 *cup white wine*
3 *tablespoons oil*
1 *medium-sized onion, finely*
chopped

2 *cups long-grained rice*
3 *hard-boiled eggs, finely*
chopped
6 *tablespoons unsalted butter*
3 *tablespoons chopped*
parsley
1 *lemon, cut into slices*

Place the salmon in a shallow flameproof dish. Sprinkle with salt and pepper and add the wine and approximately one and a half cups of water. Poach gently until the salmon is cooked (approximately 5 minutes) and remove from heat.

Pour the oil into a large frying pan and as soon as it is hot add the onion and sauté for two minutes. Add the rice and keep stirring with a wooden spoon just until it becomes translucent. Measure the wine and water in which the salmon was poached plus additional water as necessary for a total of four and a half cups of liquid. Add this to the rice. Cook, covered, over gentle heat until the rice is tender and all the water has been absorbed (about fifteen minutes). Stir with a fork from time to time to ensure the rice does not stick to the pan; if necessary, add a little more water.

Meanwhile, remove any skin and bones from the salmon and flake the fish into bite-sized pieces. Mix the fish and eggs into the cooked rice and turn into a serving dish. Before serving, cut the butter into small pieces and add it, together with the parsley, to the kedgeree. Season to taste with salt and pepper and decorate with the lemon slices.

6 SERVINGS

Brandade of Smoked Mackerel

George Perry-Smith is considered by many to be one of the fathers of new British cooking. Back in 1951, when he opened his restaurant, the Hole in the Wall, in Bath, it quickly became something of a *cause célèbre* and a place of pilgrimage for enthusiastic and desperate eaters who were willing to drive hundreds of miles for the chance to experience great cooking. The restaurant also became a kind of training school for many of the new, younger British chefs who are now so much in evidence. Today, Mr. Perry-Smith, together with his partner, Heather Crosbie, holds forth at the Riverside, a restaurant with a few rooms for overnight guests in Helford, Cornwall. People, still gladly, travel miles out of their way to eat at his table and this recipe is typical of his wonderfully eclectic attitude to food—local smoked mackerel, cooked according to a French method and served with a dill cream originating from Scandinavia and a cucumber sambal from India.

12 *ounces Puff Pastry (see*
 page 46)
½ *pound smoked mackerel*
 2 *cloves garlic*
 Salt
¼ *cup olive oil*

¼ *cup milk*
 Freshly ground black
 pepper
 1 *teaspoon lemon juice*
 1 *egg yolk, beaten with a*
 little water

SAMBAL

1 cucumber, peeled and
   diced
1 small onion, finely chopped
1 stalk celery, finely diced
   Cayenne pepper
1 tablespoon chopped parsley
   About ⅓ cup olive oil
   Lemon juice to taste
   Salt

DILL CREAM

1 cup heavy cream
2 tablespoons chopped dill
¼ teaspoon lemon juice
   Salt
   Freshly ground black
   pepper

Roll out the pastry and cut into three-inch rounds. Chill in the refrigerator.

Remove any skin or bones from the smoked mackerel. Using a pestle and mortar, crush the garlic with just enough salt to make it creamy. Add the mackerel and pound it energetically to make a smooth paste—smoother than you believed possible. This step can also be done using a food processor.

Place the mackerel and garlic mixture in a pudding basin or one-quart Pyrex bowl and place the bowl in a roasting pan filled with hot but not boiling water. Place the oil in one pitcher and the milk in another. Add the oil and the milk alternately to the mackerel in small quantities, beating them in lightly but thoroughly so that the mixture stays airy and does not become sloppy. Season to taste with pepper, lemon juice and more salt if necessary. Refrigerate until the mixture is firm.

Place a small teaspoon of the mackerel mixture on each of the pastry circles. Fold over the dough and make sure that the edges are firmly sealed. Keep the patties chilled on a lightly floured cookie sheet until just before you are ready to serve them but no more than five hours.

Preheat the oven to 450°. Brush the pastries with a little of the beaten egg yolk and bake for twelve minutes.

To prepare the sambal: Mix the cucumber with the onion and celery. Sprinkle with a little cayenne pepper and the parsley. Add enough olive oil and lemon juice to make a dressing and season to taste with salt.

To prepare the dill cream: Beat the cream until it is thick. Add the chopped dill, lemon juice and salt and pepper to taste.

Allow three pastries for each person and serve with a dollop of the dill cream and sambal on the side.

6 SERVINGS

Trout Poached in Lemon and Thyme Stock

Both this recipe and the one on page 73 were given to me by Chris Oakes, an extremely accomplished young chef at the Castle Hotel in Taunton. The Castle is a large, comfortable hotel in the middle of the town, well placed for visiting nearby Wells and Salisbury. The restaurant has an exceptional wine list and the menu is kept small. No overcooked vegetables here, unless specially requested, as noted on the menu (an amusing concession to how, with the English, some things do die hard).

So often the best dishes are the simplest to prepare; the key to their success being the freshness of their ingredients. This recipe is a case in point. In giving me the cooking instructions, Chris Oakes even offered directions for how to kill and gut the trout. But even if your trout arrives in a more conventional manner, be sure to buy it as fresh as possible as it really does make a big difference.

3 *leeks, washed and trimmed*
3 *carrots, cut in half*
3 *lemons, sliced*
1 *bunch thyme leaves*
6 *shallots, coarsely chopped*
  Salt

Freshly ground black pepper
2 *cups white wine vinegar*
4 *small trout, cleaned and gutted*
1 *lemon, cut into wedges*

Place four cups of water, leeks, carrots, lemons, thyme, shallots and some salt and pepper in a large saucepan. Bring to a boil and simmer for 20 minutes.

Pour the vinegar into a shallow dish and place the trout in the vinegar for one minute on each side.

Place the fish in the gently simmering stock for about five minutes or until it is cooked. (Test by piercing with a sharp knife—it should be flaky but moist.) Remove the fish from the stock with a slotted spatula and place on a serving dish.

Cut the leeks and carrots into fine strips and use them as a garnish for the fish. Serve with lemon wedges.

4 SERVINGS

Scallop Mousse with Prawn Sauce

This is a recipe for festive occasions. It comes from Gidleigh Park, a very special country house hotel on the edge of Dartmoor, reached by a gloriously long, winding, high-banked, single-width country lane. But if Gidleigh is remote, that only adds to its charm for the countryside is as superlative as the wine list, and the food is truly memorable.

In England, scallops come with their roe still attached, so in this respect this recipe is inevitably a little different from the Gidleigh version. You might try to get a fishmonger to supply scallops and their roe. Otherwise, this is the Gidleigh dish.

½ pound bay scallops
2 ounces any white fish
    fillets
1 egg white

Salt
1 cup plus 2 tablespoons
    heavy cream
Cayenne pepper

SAUCE

1 *shallot, finely chopped*	*Pinch of thyme*
½ *pound jumbo shrimp in*	2 *cups fish stock*
their shells	1 *cup heavy cream*
2 *tablespoons brandy*	2 *tablespoons unsalted butter*
2 *tablespoons sherry*	*Salt*
1 *tablespoon tomato paste*	*Cayenne pepper*
1 *small bay leaf*	

Purée the scallops and fish with the egg white and a pinch of salt in a food processor until smooth. Transfer the mixture to a bowl and refrigerate for 30 minutes.

To prepare the sauce: Sauté the shallot in a little oil in a heavy pan. Add the shrimp and sauté them over medium-high heat just until they are lightly colored. Add the brandy and sherry and flame.

Add the tomato paste, bay leaf, thyme and fish stock. Mix well and simmer gently for 20 minutes. Blend the mixture in a blender or food processor to produce a gritty mixture. Return to the heat and simmer for another ten minutes. Pass the mixture through a fine sieve or piece of cheesecloth, pressing to extract all moisture.

Return the mixture to the pan, add one cup of cream and simmer for fifteen minutes. Reduce the heat and beat in the butter by bits. Check the seasoning. Add salt and cayenne pepper to taste. Do not allow the sauce to boil or the butter will separate from the sauce.

Preheat oven to 350°.

Twenty minutes before serving, add one cup and two tablespoons cream to the fish and egg mixture, taking care not to overbeat. Check the seasoning and adjust if necessary. Grease six individual ramekins and place a circle of waxed paper in the bottom of each. Pipe or spoon the mousse mixture into the ramekins. Cover with foil.

Place the ramekins in a large shallow pan of hot water and cook them in the preheated oven for fifteen minutes. Allow the mousse to rest for three minutes and then serve with the sauce.

6 SERVINGS

Scallop Salad

This is a slightly less grand version of a scallop salad that is served at the Castle Hotel by Christopher Oakes. It's an extremely simple way to prepare scallops but, with the exception of the first steps of the recipe, all must be done at the last minute if it is to be served warm as at the Castle. I have found, however, that it is almost as good served at room temperature.

9 *hazelnuts, finely chopped*
6 *tablespoons olive oil*
½ *pound snow peas*
3 *carrots*
1 *pound scallops (bay or sea)*

Salt
Freshly ground black pepper

Soak the chopped hazelnuts in the oil for at least six hours.

Cut off the ends of the snow peas and cut the carrots into thin julienne strips. Blanch the carrots and snow peas in a saucepan filled with salted boiling water for 40 seconds. Drain and set aside. Up to this point can be done in advance.

If using sea scallops, cut each scallop into three pieces. Drain the oil from the hazelnuts (reserve the nuts) and place the oil in a frying pan; heat the oil gently. Season the scallops with salt and pepper and place them in the oil as soon as it is sizzling hot. Sauté for fifteen seconds, then add the carrots, snow peas and hazelnuts. Mix together in the pan until the vegetables are warm. Spoon onto individual plates and serve immediately.

4 SERVINGS

Scallops with Avocado Sauce

Another recipe for scallops, this one from Gravetye Manor. The sauce can be made ahead of time, but don't begin steaming the scallops until just before serving. Wonderful with wild rice on the side.

3/4 cup fish stock
1 1/4 cups heavy cream
1/2 ripe avocado

Salt
Freshly ground black pepper
20 sea scallops

Place the fish stock and cream in a saucepan. Bring to a boil and reduce by half. Pass the avocado through a mesh sieve or purée it in a food processor.

Add the avocado to the sauce and continue to boil gently for five minutes. Season to taste with salt and pepper.

Steam the scallops in a steamer for three to four minutes and place them on a serving plate. Cover with the avocado sauce.

4 SERVINGS

Lobster and Scallop Pie

Fish pies and fish puddings have always been popular in Britain—they probably originated as an economical method for making the fish go further. Another reason for their popularity is that they make a complete course out of one dish. A traditional fish pie is covered with mashed potatoes (see my recipe in *Great British Cooking*), but for special occasions, serve this rather more elaborate pie that has a pastry crust. Some asparagus on the side is the perfect accompaniment.

6 tablespoons unsalted butter
½ pound bay scallops
1 cup sliced mushrooms
1 pound flounder or scrod
    fillets
3 tablespoons flour
1 cup fish stock or bottled
    clam juice
1 cup heavy cream
1 cup white wine

2 teaspoons lemon juice
Salt
Freshly ground black
    pepper
¼ teaspoon nutmeg
½ pound cooked lobster meat,
    cut into one-inch pieces
6 ounces Shortcrust Pastry
    (see page 64)
1 egg yolk, beaten with a
    little water

Melt half the butter in a large pan and sauté the scallops, mushrooms and fish fillets over low heat for three to four minutes. Remove the ingredients and set aside.

Add the remaining butter to the pan, stir in the flour and make a roux. Add the fish stock, cream, wine and lemon juice gradually, stirring all the time. Season to taste with salt and pepper and add the nutmeg.

Flake the sautéed fish into two-inch pieces and add them, together with the scallops, mushrooms and lobster meat, to the sauce. Transfer the mixture to a deep nine-inch pie dish.

Preheat oven to 400°.

Roll out the pastry and place over the dish, without stretching. Press down the edges over the edge of the dish with a fork and brush the pastry with the beaten egg yolk and water mixture. Make two small slits in the pastry to allow the steam to escape and bake in the preheated oven until the pastry is golden brown (about 20 to 25 minutes). Serve hot.

6 SERVINGS

Mussel and Onion Stew

Originally a Scottish dish that is reputed to date back to medieval times, this recipe bears a strong resemblance to a New England chowder. It is the only recipe I know where the mussels are served with so many onions, resulting in a combination that I think is rather more interesting than moules marinières. Perfect with a loaf of crusty bread.

4 *quarts mussels*
  (*approximately* 90
  mussels)
1¾ *cups white wine*
8 *tablespoons unsalted*
  butter
5 *medium-sized onions,*
  finely chopped
¾ *cup flour*

2 *cups milk*
  Salt
  Freshly ground black
  pepper
5 *tablespoons chopped*
  parsley
1 *cup heavy cream*
  Juice of half a lemon

Soak the mussels in salted water for 30 minutes and then scrub and beard them, discarding any that are broken or have opened.

Place the mussels in a very large saucepan or stockpot and add the wine. Bring to a boil, cover and simmer for approximately five minutes, shaking the pan from time to time, until the mussels have all opened.

Remove the pan from the heat, lift out the mussels and, when cool enough to handle, remove them from their shells. Pour any liquid from the mussels back into the liquor in the pan. Set the mussels aside and strain the liquid through a fine sieve lined with cheesecloth.

In a clean saucepan, melt the butter and add the onions. Cook over gentle heat until the onions are soft and transparent; do not brown. Add the flour, cook for one minute and then pour in the milk and as much of the mussel liquor as you need to make a smooth, slightly thick sauce. Season to taste with salt and pepper. Add the mussels, chopped parsley, cream and lemon juice and reheat briefly. Serve in bowls.

6 SERVINGS

Fish Pudding

A steamed fish pudding (also known as fish mold, a name only the English would tolerate) is a very traditional dish. In spite of its name, it is light, airy and delicate in texture; it is an excellent main course, accompanied by a sharp sauce such as the Cranberry Sauce served at the Ritz (see page 149) or Cumberland Sauce. It can also be served cold with a salad.

1 *pound white fish fillets*	¼ *teaspoon ground ginger*
1½ *cups fresh breadcrumbs*	*Salt*
4 *tablespoons unsalted*	*Freshly ground black*
butter, melted	*pepper*
Grated rind of one lemon	3 *eggs*

Remove any skin from the fish and chop into bite-sized pieces. Mix with the breadcrumbs, butter, lemon rind and ginger, and season generously with salt and pepper. Beat the eggs and then combine with the fish mixture.

Place the fish mixture into a well-greased pudding basin or Pyrex bowl that holds three cups. Cover with a large sheet of aluminum foil pleated in the middle. Secure around the edge of the bowl with string and place on a steamer rack in a large saucepan. Place enough water in the pan to reach halfway up the basin.

Cover and steam the pudding for one hour over medium heat, checking the water from time to time to make sure that it has not all evaporated.

To serve: Remove the saucepan from the heat and allow to cool for five minutes. Remove the pudding bowl from the saucepan, take off the aluminum foil cover and run a knife around the pudding. Turn out and serve.

4 SERVINGS

Fish Choucroute

Chewton Glen is one of the most elegant country hotels in England and, with its 47 rooms, one of the largest. The restaurant is formal, the food excellent. The chef, Pierre Chevillard, contributed the following recipe based on the unlikely combination of cabbage, fish and juniper berries.

4 cups sliced cabbage	Simple Parsley Sauce
1 carrot, sliced	(see page 144)
2 onions, studded with three	Salt
cloves each	Freshly ground black
4 juniper berries	pepper
1 slice streaky bacon	½ pound bass fillet
⅔ cup white wine	½ pound sole fillet or
	another white fish fillet
	10 sea scallops

Place the cabbage, carrot, onions, juniper berries, bacon and wine in a heavy-bottomed casserole. Cover and simmer gently for one and a half hours. Prepare the parsley sauce while the choucroute is cooking.

Just before serving, drain the cabbage and season to taste with salt and pepper. Cut the fish fillets into pieces approximately two inches long by one inch wide and season with salt and pepper. Sauté them, together with the scallops in a pan, for four minutes.

Mound the cabbage in the center of a serving dish and surround it with the fish. Coat the fish lightly with the parsley sauce, and serve any remaining sauce on the side.

4 TO 6 SERVINGS

Smoked Haddock and Parsley Pie

Anthony Pitt of Homewood Park, who sent me this recipe, calls it a pie, but "pie" in England is a term far more widely used than in this country. This pie is quite like a quiche. As with other recipes that use smoked haddock, it has a very distinctive flavor and makes an excellent dish for lunch or brunch, served warm with a green salad.

6 ounces Shortcrust Pastry
  (see page 64)
1 pound smoked haddock
¼ pound cooked shrimp,
  cut into pieces
3 egg yolks

3 eggs
1¼ cups heavy cream
Salt
Freshly ground black
  pepper
1 cup parsley, finely
  chopped

Roll out the pastry and use it to line a nine-inch pie dish or quiche pan. Chill in the refrigerator until ready to use.

Preheat oven to 325°.

Place the haddock in a shallow pan and cover it with boiling water. Simmer over low heat for approximately ten minutes or until the flesh is soft. Drain and flake the haddock into small pieces.

Mix the haddock with the shrimp and place in the pastry case. Beat together the egg yolks, eggs and cream. Add a little salt and pepper and pour over the haddock and shrimp. Sprinkle the parsley over the top and bake for approximately 45 minutes or until the pie is set.

4 TO 6 SERVINGS

Talbooth Soufflé

Yet another wonderful way to cook smoked haddock. In this recipe, which comes from Sam Chalmers of Le Talbooth, a half-timbered restaurant on the bank of the river Stour, near Colchester, the haddock is poached in a mushroom and white wine sauce and topped with a cheese soufflé. Not as complicated as it sounds, this dish can be used for either a first or a main course.

½ pound smoked haddock	CHEESE SOUFFLÉ
1 cup milk	
3 tablespoons unsalted butter	2 tablespoons unsalted butter
¼ cup white wine	3 tablespoons flour
1¼ cups heavy cream	1 cup milk
⅓ cup flour	1 cup grated Cheddar cheese
1 cup sliced mushrooms	Salt
Cayenne pepper	Freshly ground black pepper
Salt	4 egg yolks
	5 egg whites

Place the haddock in a shallow pan and cover with the milk. Dot one tablespoon of the butter on top of the haddock. Cover, bring to a simmer and continue to simmer gently until the haddock is tender (about ten minutes). Strain the cooking liquid and set aside. Flake the haddock into small pieces.

In a medium-sized saucepan, bring the wine and cream to a boil and reduce to approximately one cup. Melt the remaining butter in a separate saucepan and stir in the flour. Cook over gentle heat for two minutes and then slowly add the wine and cream, stirring all the time. Add enough of the fish-cooking liquid to give the sauce the consistency of whipped cream; stir in the mushrooms and simmer for three minutes. Add the pieces of flaked fish together with a pinch of cayenne and a little salt. Remove the sauce from the heat and set aside.

To prepare the soufflé: Preheat the oven to 400°. Melt the butter in a clean saucepan and add the flour. Cook for one minute and then add the milk, stirring all the time. Bring just to a boil and when the sauce has thickened, stir in the grated cheese. Season to taste with salt and pepper and beat in the egg yolks one by one. Set aside and allow to cool slightly.

In a separate bowl, beat the egg whites until stiff and fold them into the cheese sauce. Grease eight ramekins and place a little of the haddock mixture in the bottom of each. Top with the cheese soufflé and cook for ten to twelve minutes or until the soufflés have risen and set. Serve immediately.

8 SERVINGS

Game, Poultry,
Meat and
Meat Pies

Traditionally, the British have always been carnivorous. In 1817, Dr. Kitchiner, writing in *The Cook's Oracle of Health,* advised his readers never to eat less than six pounds of meat each week. (How medical advice can change!)

Roast beef, always thought of as the country's national dish, used to provide the underpinnings in most households for the full week's menu. Known as a joint and served on Sunday with roast potatoes and Yorkshire pudding, the remains would reappear minced, hashed, curried and made into sausages and meat pies during the following week. (The exception was Friday when fish would be served.)

Patterns of eating have changed since World War II, however, and the preeminence of the Sunday Joint is a thing of the past—now it is reserved for special occasions. (To begin with, few households today could afford a twelve-pound roast each week.) There is, in its place, a new emphasis on game and poultry, an increasing use of lesser-known cuts of meat as well as a continuing interest in traditional meat pies and stews. Englishmen are still carnivorous but not enough to please John Bull or even Dr. Kitchiner.

Game, Poultry, Meat and Meat Pies

Fillet of Venison with Sour Cream and Capers

Venison Vale of Avon

Sliced Loin of Venison

Breast of Pigeon in a Red Currant, Armagnac and Juniper Berry Sauce

Salad of Pigeon Breasts with Pine Nuts

Duckling Steamed with Mint

Marinated Duck

Duck Breast with Wild Mushroom Essence

Summer Chicken

Beef Milton

Steak Esterhazy

Beef with Walnuts and Celery

Avocado, Beef and Herb Salad

Steak, Kidney and Mushroom Casserole

Pot Roast Loin of Pork with Wine and Oranges

Elizabethan Pork

Pork Cutlets with Prunes and Apple in a Cider Sauce

Marbled Veal

Veal Steak with Wild Mushroom Sauce

Roast Marinated Calves' Liver Bound in Herbs Served with an Orange Sauce

Devonshire "Mutton" Hash

Lamb Shrewsbury

Meat Pies

Grasmere Lamb Pie

Dartmouth Pie

Chicken Cider Pie

Beefsteak, Kidney and Oyster Pudding

Leek and Veal Pasties

Fillet of Venison with Sour Cream and Capers

This recipe, from Anthony Pitt of Homewood Park, is excellent and very quick to prepare. The venison steaks must be quite thin, and should resemble veal scallops. In fact, veal could easily be substituted for the venison.

4 *tablespoons unsalted butter*
6 *venison steaks, one-quarter inch thick*
1 *slice bacon, finely chopped*
1 *medium-sized onion, finely chopped*
½ *cup white wine*

½ *cup chicken stock*
Grated rind and juice of two lemons
1 *cup sour cream*
Salt
Freshly ground black pepper

Melt the butter in a large frying pan and add the venison steaks. Sauté till cooked, about six minutes, turning frequently. Remove the steaks to a serving dish and keep warm.

Using the same pan, add the bacon and onion, white wine and chicken stock to the melted butter. Bring to a boil and reduce by half. Add the lemon juice, cream and capers. Check the seasoning, add salt and pepper to taste and pour over the venison steaks.

6 SERVINGS

Venison Vale of Avon

"You can get the best game in the world in England," Frank Harris wrote in his book *My Life and Loves*, "but, alas, the English always keep it until it is high, or if you prefer the truth, till it is almost rotten." He did exaggerate, but the question of how long game should be hung is one of those deep mysteries I don't pretend to understand. I do know that the best venison comes usually from young deer, as it is much less inclined to be tough.

The venison recipes all call for the venison to be cut into steaks or small fillets, thus increasing the likelihood of tenderness. This recipe is a specialty of the Priory Hotel on the outskirts of Bath, a rambling, Victorian house set in two acres of gardens that overlook the whole city. The chef is Michael Collom, an Englishman trained entirely in his native country, and this venison dish is one of his favorites. It is to be found frequently on the Priory menu.

1½ pounds saddle of venison	2 cups sliced mushrooms
1 onion, coarsely chopped	6 shallots, finely chopped
1 carrot, coarsely chopped	½ cup Madeira
1 cup red wine	2 cups dark cherries, pitted
4 tablespoons unsalted	(first-quality canned
butter	cherries in water, not
Salt	syrup, if fresh are not
Freshly ground black	available)
pepper	½ bunch watercress

Ask your butcher to bone the venison and trim off all the fat. Use the bones to make a stock with the onion, carrot and four cups of water. Simmer for two hours, strain and reduce to approximately one and a half cups of liquid. Add the red wine and set aside. (This can be done a day ahead of time but be sure to refrigerate the stock overnight.)

Cut the venison fillet into about eighteen medallions and flatten them slightly. Heat two-thirds of the butter in a large frying pan over medium-high heat. Season the medallions generously with salt and pepper. Sauté in the butter for half a minute on each side. Remove from the pan and keep warm.

Place the mushrooms and shallots in the frying pan and sauté for a few minutes. Add the stock and wine mixture and the Madeira and reduce until the consistency is quite syrupy. Add the remaining butter in small pieces. Check the seasoning and add the cherries. Heat through.

Arrange the venison on a serving dish and surround it with the sauce. Decorate with the watercress.

4 TO 6 SERVINGS

Sliced Loin of Venison

This venison recipe comes from the Castle, that oasis of comfort and good cooking in Taunton. The flavors of the cranberries and the apples complement the venison exceptionally well, and although the recipe calls for a fairly large number of ingredients and requires good organizational skills, it is in fact not all that complicated to prepare.

1½ *pounds loin of venison*
  1 *carrot, coarsely chopped*
  1 *large onion, coarsely*
    chopped
  7 *cups beef stock*
 10 *juniper berries*
  2 *tablespoons tomato paste*
  4 *tablespoons unsalted*
    butter
    Salt

Freshly ground black
pepper
2 *heaping tablespoons fresh*
  cranberries
2 *heaping tablespoons*
  honey
1 *apple, peeled and cored*
2 *tablespoons brown sugar*
¼ *cup Calvados*

Have your butcher bone the venison and cut it into six steaks. Place the venison bones, carrot and onion in a large saucepan. Add the stock, juniper berries and tomato paste. Bring to a boil and skim the top. Leave to simmer for two and one-half hours. Strain and reduce until about three cups of the liquid remain. Leave to cool. (This part of the recipe can be done a day ahead of time. If preparing the stock in advance, cool and then refrigerate overnight.)

Melt half the butter in a large frying pan and add the venison steaks. Season generously with salt and pepper. Sauté the steaks quickly, taking care not to overcook. Set aside and keep warm.

Place the cranberries and the honey in a small pan and simmer for three to four minutes. Using a melon scoop, cut balls out of the apple and add them to the sauce. In a separate pan, melt the sugar and the Calvados. Bring the mixture to a boil and add the remaining butter in small pieces.

Serve the steaks on separate plates, placing them on top of the sauce, with the cranberry and apple mixture served on the side.

6 SERVINGS

Breast of Pigeon in a Red Currant, Armagnac and Juniper Berry Sauce

Until the nineteenth century, pigeons were classified as poultry, and having one's own dovecote was as common as keeping one's own hens. Mrs. Beeton gives her readers elaborate instructions for keeping a dovecote clean, and explains the necessity for painting the perches white (a pigeon's favorite color) and having the front of the dovecote face southwest. She also tackles the question of breeding and points out that, if well supplied with food, a pigeon can be bred at least eight times a year. This fact helps to explain the frequency of pigeons in old English cuisine.

Although today pigeons are classified as game birds and are certainly less abundant than they were, they are starting to be found more and more often on the menu. And in many places, excellent pigeons—or squabs—are being bred for the table. This recipe from the Peat Inn is particularly delicious.

4 *pigeons or squabs*
1 *carrot, diced*
1 *small onion, finely chopped*
1 *stalk celery, chopped*
¼ *cup mushrooms, finely sliced*
6 *tablespoons red wine*
1¼ *cups chicken stock*
  Salt
  Freshly ground black pepper

SAUCE

¾ *cup red wine*
1 *tablespoon red currant jelly*
1 *tablespoon wine vinegar*
8 *tablespoons unsalted butter*
6 *juniper berries*
¼ *cup Armagnac*
  Salt
  Freshly ground black pepper

Remove the legs from the pigeons.

Place all the vegetables in a large, deep saucepan; add the wine and the stock, bring to a boil and simmer for eight minutes. Sprinkle the vegetables with a little salt and pepper

and place the pigeons on top of the vegetables. (The liquid
should cover the vegetables but not the pigeons.) Cover the
pan and bring back to a boil. Simmer for another ten minutes but check to make sure that the liquid does not evapo-
rate. Test the pigeons to see if they are cooked. The breasts
should be pink but should "give" to the touch. Turn off the
heat and leave until ready to carve.

To prepare the sauce: Place the wine, red currant jelly
and vinegar in a small, wide saucepan. Bring to a boil and
reduce until the mixture is almost a syrup, stirring occasionally while it is reducing. Pour off the stock from cooking the pigeons and vegetables and strain and add it to the
sauce. Continue to reduce until the sauce is syrupy, then add
the juniper berries. Return to a boil and whisk in the butter
in small pieces. Pour in the Armagnac and check the consistency of the sauce. Reduce further if it seems too thin,
add a little stock if it is too thick. Finally, check the seasoning. Add salt and pepper to taste.

To serve: Lift out the pigeons from the saucepan and
with a sharp knife slice off their breasts in one piece. Slice
each breast into fine strips. Serve the sliced meat surrounded
by the sauce.

6 SERVINGS

Salad of Pigeon Breasts with Pine Nuts

The inscription over the entrance of Hambleton Hall, near Oakham, reads *Fay Ce Que Voudras* ("do as you please"), and Nicholas Gill, who is the chef at this most elegant and comfortable country house hotel, has taken the invitation of this motto to develop an inventive and distinctly individual menu that draws heavily on local ingredients. The son of a well-known television producer, Gill is not yet 30 years old but, having trained in both England and France, he seems to possess culinary wisdom far beyond his years.

Praise for Hambleton's ambience, comfort and extraordinarily good food is due in equal measure to Tim and Stefa Hart, the proprietors. They seem instinctively to understand the art of gracious living and follow a simple unencumbered rule for their guests—to provide the very best. The result is a hotel that has become one of the most desirable escape points from London.

The culinary style at Hambleton does not lend itself easily to the skills of the nonprofessional. This pigeon salad, however, although it does call for some exotic ingredients, is not too hard to execute for a special occasion. Serve it with crutsy bread and a hearty Beaujolais.

A selection of salad ingredients such as chicory, Boston lettuce, radicchio, dandelion leaves (enough for four people)
2 *pigeons or squabs*
1 *carrot, finely chopped*
1 *stalk celery, finely chopped*
1 *small onion, finely chopped*
1 *bouquet garni (thyme, bay leaf and parsley)*

¼ *cup white wine*
1½ *cups beef stock*
2 *shallots, finely chopped*
3 *tablespoons wine vinegar*
2 *teaspoons red currant jelly*
2 *tablespoons walnut oil*
½ *teaspoon fresh thyme*
Salt
Freshly ground black pepper
2 *tablespoons pine nuts*

Wash all the salad ingredients, drain, wrap them in cloth or paper towels and place them in the refrigerator. Remove the breast meat from the pigeons and set aside. Coarsely chop the carcasses and place them in a saucepan together with the carrot, celery and onion. Add the bouquet garni and white wine. Cover and cook over medium heat for five minutes. Add the stock, cover and allow to simmer for two hours to extract all the flavor from the pigeons and the vegetables.

Strain into a clean saucepan, pushing down on the solids with the back of a spoon in order to extract all the juices. Return to the heat and bring to a simmer. Reduce until a syrupy consistency is obtained. Skim any impurities off the surface of the sauce. Place the shallots in another saucepan, add the vinegar and simmer until the vinegar has completely evaporated. Add the reduced pigeon stock and the red currant jelly. Finally whisk in one tablespoon of oil.

Place the remaining oil in a frying pan, season the pigeon breasts with the thyme and with salt and pepper. Fry them for approximately three minutes on each side until they are cooked but still pink inside. Remove the pigeon breasts onto a clean board and slice them as thin as possible. Arrange the salad leaves on four plates, sprinkle the pine nuts on top and place the slices of pigeon in the middle of each plate. Spoon the sauce over both the pigeon and the salad leaves and serve immediately.

4 SERVINGS

Duckling Steamed with Mint

Shaun Hill is one of the founding members of Country Chefs Seven, a group of young English chefs who banded together a few years ago to demonstrate that being French is not an essential prerequisite for a talented, serious chef. Before opening his own restaurant, Hill's in Stratford-Upon-Avon, Shaun Hill was head chef at the Lygon Arms in Broadway— that showpiece town in the heart of the Cotswold country— where I was lucky enough to be served this recipe. The steaming or sweating of the duck makes it very tender and not the least bit dry.

1 *duck* (3 to 4 *pounds*)	1 *cup white wine*
Salt	1 *large bunch mint leaves*
Freshly ground black	12 *tablespoons unsalted butter*
pepper	2 *teaspoons lemon juice*

Place the duck on a large sheet of aluminum foil. Pull out any loose fat around the neck or large cavity and discard. Rub salt and pepper over the duck, and moisten with a little of the wine. Chop the mint and rub half of it over the duck, placing some of it in the large cavity. Wrap the foil tightly around the duck.

Place a steaming rack in a large saucepan and pour in two inches of water. Place the duck on the rack. Bring the water to a boil and cover. Simmer for one hour, checking from time to time to make sure that the water has not evaporated.

Remove the duck from the steamer and allow to rest for fifteen minutes.

Preheat the oven to 400°. Lift the duck out of the aluminum foil and drain off and reserve any fat that has accumulated for future use. Place the duck in a roasting pan and cook in the oven for half an hour, basting from time to time and removing excess fat so that it does not burn in the roasting pan. As an alternative to roasting, the duck can be carved into pieces and fried until crisp, on the skin side in some of the fat reserved from steaming.

While the duck is in the last stages of cooking, place the remaining chopped mint and wine in a shallow saucepan. Bring to a boil and reduce by half. Continuing to cook it over gentle heat, beat in the butter in small pieces until the sauce thickens. Add the lemon juice and season to taste. Serve the sauce with the duck.

6 SERVINGS

Marinated Duck

Salted duck, where the duck is rubbed with coarse salt and left to marinate for several days before being cooked, is a traditional Welsh specialty. Lady Augusta Llanover, who came from Lincolnshire but was a champion of everything Welsh, includes a recipe for salted duck in her book, *The First Principles of Good Cookery*, which was published in 1867. She recommends salting the duck for three days, then boiling and serving it with an onion sauce.

This recipe from Milton Sandford is a modified version: the duck is marinated for a considerably shorter time and is roasted rather than boiled. It is nevertheless a recipe with excellent traditional antecedents. Serve this dish with Green Pepper Sauce (see page 143) as they do at Milton Sandford.

1 *duck* (3 *to* 4 *pounds*)	3 *teaspoons sea salt*
1 *teaspoon paprika*	2 *shallots, finely chopped*

Remove the breasts with the wings attached to them from the duck and place them skin side down in a shallow dish. Rub the paprika and the salt all over them and sprinkle with the chopped shallots. Place in the refrigerator, uncovered, for 24 hours. Remove the legs whole from the duck, wrap them in foil and also refrigerate until ready for use.

Preheat the oven to 425°. Discard any liquid that has accumulated around the duck breasts and blot the breasts dry before placing them, together with the legs, in a roasting pan.

Roast for 20 minutes (due to the salt in the marinade, the breasts will remain pink; do not overcook). Slice the breasts into several pieces, arrange on a serving dish with the legs and serve.

4 SERVINGS

Duck Breast with Wild Mushroom Essence

Gidleigh Park has become something of a code word among English culinary cognoscenti—even I feel a certain reluctance to let too many people in on the secret that there exists deep in the remote countryside of Devonshire this extraordinary country house hotel, owned and managed furthermore by Paul and Kay Henderson, an American couple, both of whom are perfectionists and dream of comfort and cuisine rather than expansion and annexes. When the hotel first opened a few years ago, Kay Henderson did all the cooking herself; now it is in the hands of John Webber, a delightfully unassuming young man who cheerfully admits that prior to his seven-year apprenticeship with Anton Mosimann at the Dorchester in London, he possessed a blissful ignorance of any of the finer aspects of food. He was, obviously, a good pupil: the food at Gidleigh is impeccable and this dish is one tempting example.

½ ounce dried cèpes
½ ounce dried morels
½ cup dry white wine
½ cup chicken consommé
3 cups veal stock
½ teaspoon tomato paste
½ teaspoon arrowroot

2 small ducks, with legs and
    wings removed and the
    breasts on the bone
1 tablespoon honey
1 teaspoon prepared English
    mustard
4 fresh wild mushrooms,
    coarsely chopped

Place the dried mushrooms, wine and chicken consommé in a pan and bring to a boil. Remove from the heat and allow to stand at least two hours or overnight if possible.

Preheat the oven to 425°.

Remove the mushrooms from the consommé-wine mixture, add the veal stock and bring to a boil. Reduce the sauce by one-third of its volume. Beat in the tomato paste and thicken with the arrowroot. Keep warm over low heat.

Place the duck breasts skin side down in a roasting pan and roast in the preheated oven for ten minutes. Mix together the honey and the mustard, turn the breasts over and brush with the glaze. Cook for another ten minutes, brushing every four minutes with the glaze.

Add the fresh mushrooms to the sauce and simmer for five minutes. Remove the duck breast from the bone and slice it with the skin on. Brush any remaining glaze over the duck slices and serve with the sauce.

4 SERVINGS

Summer Chicken

Another recipe from Imogen Skirving, who, as a participant in the At Home Country Holidays program, frequently entertains Americans at Langar Hall, her home in Nottinghamshire. Cooking with yogurt rather than sour cream has become very popular in the last few years; for some reason sour cream is much harder to obtain in England. This recipe uses yogurt to counterbalance the hot spices in which the chicken has been marinated. Serve with lots of rice.

Juice of one lemon
3 tablespoons olive oil
2 cloves garlic, crushed
1 teaspoon turmeric
3 teaspoons ground or
   powdered cumin

1 large handful fresh mint
   leaves, finely chopped
6 large chicken breasts,
   boned
¾ cup yogurt
   Coriander leaves for
   garnish

Place all the ingredients except the chicken and the yogurt in a food processor and blend to make a paste. Rub this mixture over the chicken and leave it to marinate for at least one hour.

Preheat the oven to 350°.

Place the chicken in its marinade in a flameproof casserole, cover and bake for 40 minutes or until the chicken is tender. Remove the chicken from the oven, set aside and keep warm. Bring the juices remaining in the baking pan to a boil and reduce to approximately one and a half cups. Remove from heat and stir in the yogurt. Place the chicken pieces on a platter, pour the sauce over and serve with fresh coriander leaves.

6 SERVINGS

Beef Milton

Victorian England held horseradish in the highest regard. It
was believed to "promote appetite and excite the digestive
organs" (Mrs. Beeton), and was always served with roast
beef and used as a garnish for fish. Pungent and sharp, fresh
horseradish has a taste all its own. In this recipe, which
comes from Richard Sandford of Milton Sandford, it is
quickly pan fried with strips of sirloin steak and then laced
with cream.

1½ pounds sirloin steak
2 tablespoons vegetable oil
2 shallots, finely chopped
2 teaspoons freshly grated
 horseradish (if unavail-
 able, substitute three teaspoons prepared horse-
radish from a new jar)
5 tablespoons heavy cream
Salt
Freshly ground black
pepper

Cut the beef into thin strips approximately two inches in
length and remove any fat or gristle. If possible, cut the
beef so that the grain runs across the width rather than the
length of the strips.

Place the oil in a large frying pan and heat gently until
it starts to smoke. Add the shallots and beef to the pan. Turn
the heat all the way up and fry, constantly shaking or stirring the beef so that it doesn't stick or burn. When the meat
is browned all over but not overcooked, in about three or four
minutes, add the horseradish and cream and season to taste
with salt and pepper. Keep stirring until the cream is about
to come to a boil, remove and serve immediately.

4 SERVINGS

Steak Esterhazy

The Lake District is famous for its scenery, its walks and its connections with Wordsworth. It also has one of the greatest concentrations of good food and comfortable places to stay in the whole of England. The Sharrow Bay Hotel, which has been owned and managed for over 35 years by Francis Coulson and Brian Sack, is probably the best known in the District and with good reason. Visitors are offered an amazingly hospitable welcome and dinner is an obligatory six-course affair, beginning with a dazzling array of first courses, then fish, a sorbet, a choice of entrées, dessert and a spectacular cheese board. One of the charms of dinner at Sharrow Bay is that Francis Coulson, who is in charge of all the cooking, is apt to emerge from the kitchen, clad in white from head to toe, to chat with guests, gauge their response to a particular dish and exhort the weaker eaters not to flag.

Steak Esterhazy is regularly on the menu. The dish originally came from a Viennese family of that name and it is a recipe that Mr. Coulson has been re-creating in his kitchen for many years.

Salt	*⅛ teaspoon allspice*
Freshly ground black	*3 bay leaves*
pepper	*4 peppercorns*
2 pounds sirloin or chuck	*1 strip lemon peel*
steak in one piece	*4 slices bacon, chopped*
Flour to dredge the steak	*2 tablespoons chopped*
3 tablespoons oil	*parsley*
2 medium-sized onions,	*3 tablespoons white wine*
finely chopped	*vinegar*
2 cloves garlic, chopped	*½ cup heavy cream*
2 tablespoons flour	*Juice of half a lemon*
2 cups beef stock	*Parsley for garnish*
2 carrots, finely chopped	

Rub a generous amount of salt and pepper into the steak and dredge it lightly in flour.

Heat the oil in a large frying pan that has a cover. Add

the steak and brown it quickly on both sides. Remove and add the onions and garlic. Cook for two minutes without browning and then stir in the flour. Pour in the stock slowly, stirring all the time, and bring the sauce to a boil. Add the carrots, allspice, bay leaves, peppercorns, lemon peel, bacon, parsley and vinegar. Put back the steak, cover the frying pan and simmer for 50 minutes.

Remove the steak. Strain the sauce through a sieve and skim off any fat. Add the cream and lemon juice, season to taste and reheat briefly without boiling. Slice the steak and place it on a serving dish. Cover with the sauce and sprinkle with parsley.

4 TO 6 SERVINGS

Beef with Walnuts and Celery

This recipe comes from Noreen Hope, another of the hosts who participate in At Home Country Holidays. Mrs. Hope lives at Blunts Chase, a Georgian farmhouse that adjoins Epping Forest and yet is only fourteen miles from the center of London. She offers her guests what she likes to call "good home cooking" and tells me that this is one of her recipes that most regularly returns home with American visitors.

1½ pounds chuck steak, cut
    into cubes
    Salt
    Freshly ground black
    pepper
¼ cup flour
2 tablespoons vegetable oil
2 large onions, finely
    chopped
1 clove garlic, crushed
1 cup red wine

1½ cups beef stock
2 cups sliced mushrooms
1 bouquet garni (thyme,
    bay leaf and parsley)
2 tablespoons unsalted
    butter
½ cup shelled walnuts
2 stalks celery, finely diced
2 teaspoons grated fresh
    orange peel

Sprinkle the meat with salt and pepper and dredge in all but one tablespoon of the flour.

Preheat the oven to 300°.

Heat the oil in a heavy flameproof casserole, add the meat and brown it on all sides. Add the onions and garlic and continue to cook until they are soft and transparent. Add the remaining flour, cook for one minute and then pour in the wine and stock, stirring all the time. Bring to a simmer, add the mushrooms and the bouquet garni and season with more salt and pepper.

Cover the dish and cook in the oven for one and one-quarter hours. If the stew seems very runny, continue to cook it uncovered for another half hour, otherwise keep it covered and cook for another half hour.

Shortly before serving, melt the butter in a shallow pan over gentle heat. Add the walnuts and celery. Cook gently for five minutes and then add the orange peel. Remove the meat from the oven, check the seasoning, spread the walnuts and celery on top of the meat and serve.

4 TO 6 SERVINGS

Avocado, Beef and Herb Salad

The Hole in the Wall, a small restaurant in the center of Bath, achieved almost legendary status when it first opened many years ago under the ownership of George Perry-Smith. In those days, finding a really good meal outside of London was still very much of a feat and Mr. Perry-Smith's table was considered to be worth a considerable detour. His restaurant also became a training ground for many of today's younger generation of chefs. Alas for Bath, Mr. Perry-Smith has since removed to Cornwall and the restaurant changed hands. For some time there were murmurings and discontent voiced by former patrons. However, the Hole in the Wall has recently reopened under the management of Tim and Angela Cumming and Bath is again in much better spirits. This recipe comes from the Cummings and is a perfect summer dish. Although it calls for steak or London broil, cold roast beef can also be used.

1½ pounds steak or London broil
1 avocado
4 to 6 lettuce leaves
¼ teaspoon chopped fresh thyme
¼ teaspoon chopped fresh basil
¼ teaspoon chopped fresh parsley
2 tablespoons vinaigrette (see in recipe page 139)

Broil the steak for about twelve minutes or until it is rare to pink and allow to cool. Reserve any accumulated juices.

Slice the steak into long thin strips. Peel the avocado and slice it lengthwise into strips. Cut the lettuce leaves into fine ribbons and sprinkle on a plate. Arrange the avocado and beef in alternating strips over the lettuce. Sprinkle the herbs on top. Remove and discard any fat from the beef juices and beat the juices into the French dressing; dribble over the salad and serve.

4 TO 6 SERVINGS

Steak, Kidney and Mushroom Casserole

This is a twentieth-century, time-saving variation of that most English of all dishes—steak and kidney pie. This recipe requires absolutely no culinary flare or expertise, can be made in advance, tastes better the longer it waits to be eaten and is one of the few recipes I know that does not turn the cook into a monster should the guests be late.

2 medium-sized onions, finely chopped
2 tablespoons vegetable oil
1 tablespoon flour
2 pounds chuck steak, cut into cubes
½ pound veal kidneys, cut into half-inch pieces
Vegetable oil
1 bottle Guinness (6½ ounces)
3 tablespoons Worcestershire sauce
Salt
Freshly ground black pepper
1 bay leaf
½ teaspoon thyme
½ teaspoon rosemary
2 cups mushrooms, coarsely sliced

Preheat the oven to 300°.

Fry the onions in the oil in a frying pan until soft and then transfer them to a large casserole. Coat the steak and kidneys with the flour and brown the meat in small batches in the frying pan. (Add a little more oil if necessary.) Mix the meat with the onions in the casserole and pour in the Guinness and the Worcestershire sauce. Add a generous amount of salt and pepper, together with the bay leaf and the herbs.

Cover the casserole and place in the oven. Cook for two hours. Remove the cover and cook for another hour. Lightly sauté the mushrooms in a little oil and add them to the casserole. Cook for 30 minutes more. If the sauce gets too thick and sticky, add a little more beer or water. Adjust the seasoning before serving.

6 SERVINGS

Pot Roast Loin of Pork with Wine and Oranges

Michael's Nook is one of the newer of the extremely comfortable country house hotels in the Lake District. The food is of an exceptional quality with small menus that are imaginative and inventive. The cooking is in the hands of two very young chefs, Paul Vidic and Philip Vickery, and their reputation is now such that booking in advance is almost essential.

This recipe is from Michael's Nook and comes up with the surprising combination of oranges and pork. The result is most satisfying.

3 *pounds boned loin of pork*
  (*ask your butcher to give*
  you the bones chopped
  into small pieces)
3 *oranges*
1 *clove garlic, crushed*
  Salt
  Freshly ground black pepper
3 *tablespoons parsley,*
  finely chopped

1 *medium-sized onion*
1 *carrot*
½ *stalk celery*
1 *leek*
1½ *cups dry white wine*
1 *cup chicken stock*
½ *cup heavy cream*

Preheat the oven to 350°.

Grate the zest off one of the oranges and reserve; peel and cut the orange into segments and set aside.

Place the pork bones in the bottom of a large flameproof roasting pan. Lay the pork flat, season the inside with garlic, salt, pepper, orange zest and one tablespoon of parsley. Roll the pork into a joint or roast and tie with string to secure it. Season the outside with salt and pepper.

Dice the onion, carrot, celery and leek and place them in the roasting pan. Place the pork on top of the vegetables and roast in the oven for 25 minutes.

Remove the pan from the oven and pour in one cup of

wine, the juice of the remaining oranges and the chicken stock. Cover the pan with a large sheet of aluminum foil and seal the edges tightly. Place over a medium-high flame until the liquid comes to a boil, turn down the oven to 325° and return the covered pan to the oven to cook for another 45 minutes.

Remove the pork from the pan, strain the juices into a wide-bottomed saucepan and bring to a rolling boil on top of the stove. Continue to boil until the liquid has reduced to approximately one cup. Skim off any fat or impurities, turn down the heat and add the cream. Reheat gently but do not allow to boil.

Slice the pork and place on individual plates or a large serving dish. Place an orange segment on each slice of meat, pour over the sauce, sprinkle with the remaining chopped parsley and serve.

4 TO 6 SERVINGS

Elizabethan Pork

The Elizabethans lived before forks came into wide use, and they enjoyed handling their food directly. Many dishes were served in "ragoo" form, however, so that they could be easily eaten with a spoon. In those days meat was frequently cooked with fruit and spices as a way to hide any spoilage. This Elizabethan-style recipe, which comes from Michael Smith, is marvelously spicy, and ideal for large parties as it is one of those dishes that tastes all the better for being made a day or so in advance. The quantities given here are for twelve persons, or you can use half and freeze the rest for later use.

3½ pounds boneless stewing
    pork
4 tablespoons vegetable oil
¼ cup flour
2 medium-sized onions,
    chopped
3 stalks celery, diced
    Vegetable oil
1 cup dried apricots
2 large green apples, cored
    and cut into pieces
1 cup pitted dates
1 cup seedless raisins
    Grated rind and juice of
    one lemon
    Grated rind and juice of
    one orange

1 tablespoon honey
2 cups red wine
1 teaspoon marjoram
1 teaspoon thyme
1 teaspoon cinnamon
1 teaspoon mace
1 teaspoon freshly ground
    black pepper
1 teaspoon curry powder
3 cloves garlic, crushed
    Salt
1 cup chopped walnuts
1 tablespoon unsalted
    butter
2 oranges, broken into
    segments

Preheat the oven to 325°.

Trim off any excess fat from the meat and cut into half-inch cubes. Heat the oil in a large frying pan and, while it is getting hot, dredge the meat in the flour. Sauté the meat in the oil until it is lightly browned. This is best done a little at a time, transferring the browned meat to an ovenproof casserole as ready. Next, brown the onions and celery in the same pan, adding a little more oil if necessary. Transfer the vegetables to the casserole.

Sprinkle any remaining flour onto the meat. Coarsely chop the apricots, apple pieces and dates, and add them, together with the raisins, rind and juice of the lemon and orange. Stir in the honey and wine and add the herbs and spices, garlic and a teaspoon of salt. Cover and cook in the oven for three hours, stirring from time to time. Add more salt if needed.

Before serving, fry the walnuts in butter until they are hot and scatter them, together with the segmented oranges, over the dish.

12 SERVINGS

Pork Cutlets with Prunes and Apple in a Cider Sauce

A contemporary pig bred for eating bears little resemblance to the wild boars that used to abound in the forests of England and provide sport as well as food for generations of hunters. In medieval times, pork in puddings, pies and sausages was extremely popular. Applesauce is traditionally served with pork in England but this recipe, from the Castle Hotel in Taunton, combines apples and prunes with Calvados to make a sauce that is rather more interesting.

16 *pieces of turned apple*
  (*see note*)
16 *pitted prunes*
 8 *tablespoons unsalted butter*
 4 *pork cutlets*
 4 *tablespoons dark brown*
  sugar

4 *tablespoons Calvados*
2½ *cups country cider*
½ *cup chicken stock*
½ *cup heavy cream*
  Salt
  Freshly ground black
  pepper

Stuff the bits of apple into the prunes and set aside. In a frying pan, melt half the butter and sauté the pork cutlets over gentle heat until they are cooked. While they are cooking, melt the sugar and the Calvados in a small pan and add the stuffed prunes. Simmer gently over low heat until the cutlets are ready—about 15 to 20 minutes.

To make the sauce: Place the cider and the chicken stock in a saucepan and reduce to a scant cup. Add the heavy cream and remove from heat. Whisk in the remaining butter in small pieces and season to taste with the salt and pepper if needed.

To serve, spoon a little of the sauce onto each plate and place a cutlet on top of the sauce. Arrange four prunes around each cutlet and glaze the top of the cutlet with a spoonful of the Calvados and sugar mixture.

4 SERVINGS

Note: To make "turned" apple pieces, peel, core and cut the apple into 16 segments. With a sharp paring knife shape the segments into pieces about one inch long that look like elongated, tapered eggs.

Marbled Veal

As the name implies this dish has the look of marble when sliced and was just one of a number of ways the Georgians fancied to make a dish look attractive. There are a number of recipes for this excellent English answer to the French terrine. This one comes from Michael Smith, who, through his cookbooks, articles and lectures, has done so much to reinstate traditional dishes that had all but vanished from the national cuisine. Serve Marbled Veal thinly sliced with Cumberland Sauce as a first course or with a green salad as a cold main dish in summer. It can easily be made one or two days in advance and in fact improves with time.

¾ pound ground veal
¾ pound ground loin of pork
¼ pound extra-fat ground
    loin of pork
  Grated rind of one lemon
2 tablespoons chopped
    parsley
1 tablespoon chopped chives
    or scallions
  Salt

Freshly ground black
    pepper
2 eggs
½ pound cooked tongue
 2 uncooked, boned chicken
    breasts
½ cup Madeira
½ packet unflavored gelatin
    (1 teaspoon)

Mix together the ground veal and pork with the lemon rind, parsley, chives or scallions and a generous amount of salt and pepper. Beat the eggs and blend them in to bind the mixture.

Cut the tongue and chicken breasts into small cubes—about one-half inch—and mix them with the other meats. Warm the Madeira and dissolve the gelatin in it; then work it well into the meats.

Preheat the oven to 350°.

Butter an 8½- by 4½-inch loaf pan and fill it with the mixture. Cover the top with aluminum foil and stand the pan in another pan that has enough water in it to come half-way up the sides of the loaf pan.

Cook for one and a half hours in the oven. Allow to cool, then cover with a weight and chill in the refrigerator for at least two hours before serving. When ready to use, run a knife around the sides and gently turn the loaf out onto a serving dish. Trim off any fat that may have congealed and serve in thin slices.

6 SERVINGS

Veal Steak with Wild Mushroom Sauce

John Webber, who is now responsible for the marvelous food at Gidleigh Park, looks to be the kind of man who would be happiest downing seven pints at the pub, and much more likely to be discussing the finer points of dart-throwing than haute cuisine. In point of fact, he enjoys spending his spare time combing the countryside in search of new sources of farm-laid eggs and will discourse happily for hours on the merits of lesser-known farm-made cheeses. Local mushrooms are another passion and when they can be found, this recipe appears on the menu at Gidleigh.

½ cup button mushrooms
1 cup wild mushrooms
   (chanterelles or cèpes)
3 tablespoons unsalted butter
⅔ cup white wine
2 shallots, finely chopped
⅔ cup veal or chicken stock

1¼ cups heavy cream
4 veal steaks or veal chops
Salt
Freshly ground black
   pepper
Vegetable oil
2 tablespoons chopped
   parsley

Slice the mushrooms and sweat them in one tablespoon of the butter in a covered saucepan for approximately four minutes. Set aside.

Place the white wine and the shallots in a shallow pan. Bring to a boil and reduce by half. Add the stock, return to a boil, add the cream and simmer slowly, reducing by one-quarter.

While the sauce is reducing, season the veal steaks with salt and pepper and sauté them in a little oil just until cooked, about three to four minutes on each side.

Add the mushrooms to the sauce. Bring to a boil for a few seconds, whisk in the remaining butter, cut into pieces, and check the seasoning.

Place each steak on a separate plate, pour the sauce over, heaping the mushrooms on the steaks, and sprinkle with parsley.

4 SERVINGS

Roast Marinated Calves' Liver Bound in Herbs Served with an Orange Sauce

Liver dishes are almost nonexistent in early cookery manuals. One has to conclude that with the exception of liver and bacon, always a popular dish, calves' liver was mostly used, along with the rest of the offal, for sausages, forcemeat and meat puddings. However, today it can frequently be found on menus. This recipe comes from Michael Quinn, who has earned a dazzling reputation for his food first at Gravetye, then at the Ritz and now at Ettington Park.

1½ pounds calves' liver, cleaned and with the filament removed
Juice of ten oranges or 2 cups orange juice
6 shallots, chopped
1 clove garlic, crushed
2 sprigs parsley, chopped
2 sprigs thyme, chopped, or ½ teaspoon dried thyme
3 basil leaves, chopped
½ teaspoon sage

½ teaspoon rosemary
½ teaspoon tarragon
Parsley for garnish

SAUCE

2½ cups marinade juice
1 cup veal or chicken stock
2 tablespoons unsalted butter
1 teaspoon chopped fresh mixed herbs (chosen from above)
Grated rind of one orange

Place the liver with the orange juice, shallots, garlic, parsley, thyme and basil in a dish. Cover and allow to marinate for 24 hours.

One hour prior to serving, remove the liver from the marinade and pat off excess liquid. Reserve the marinade. Combine the sage, rosemary and tarragon and use them to coat the liver. Wrap it in a piece of very fine cheesecloth. Secure it with string but don't tie it too tightly. Preheat the oven to 400°. Roast the liver for ten minutes and set aside.

To make the sauce: While the liver is roasting, reduce the marinade to one-third of its volume, add the stock and continue to boil until the liquor has reduced again to one-third its volume. Remove any scum and excess fat and add the butter in small pieces. Add the herbs and orange rind just before serving.

Remove the string and cheesecloth from the liver and slice thin. Allow about three slices per person and place on individual plates or on one serving dish on top of the sauce. Garnish with parsley.

4 TO 6 SERVINGS

Devonshire "Mutton" Hash

In a country where the full week's menu of dishes was once planned around the leftovers from Sunday's joint of meat, hashes have always held an honored place. Mrs. Beeton refers rather charmingly to them as "cold meat cookery." She provides several hash recipes for her readers as do both Hannah Glasse and Eliza Acton.

Today, hashes are still popular and can be delicious. Ideally, this recipe should be made with hard English cider but I find it works fine with American country cider. (Supermarket apple juice is really not an acceptable substitute. Should you be unable to obtain any country cider, substitute Guinness.) Serve this hash with homemade fried-bread croutons (use the hot buttered toast on page 56), and a green bean salad. This preparation recalls a traditional treatment of leftover mutton, but it is also ideal for lamb, especially from the leg.

8 tablespoons unsalted butter
7 medium-sized carrots,
   thinly sliced in rounds
4 medium-sized onions,
   thinly sliced into rings
½ teaspoon chopped fresh
   rosemary
½ teaspoon chopped fresh
   tarragon
½ teaspoon ground coriander
¼ teaspoon nutmeg

Freshly ground black
   pepper
Salt
2 tablespoons flour
2 cups beef or lamb stock
1 cup country cider or
   Guinness
1 pound cooked lamb, cut
   into half-inch cubes
1 clove garlic, finely
   chopped
Parsley for garnish

Melt half the butter in a large pan and add the carrots and
onions, sautéing them over low heat for about four minutes.
Add the herbs and a generous amount of pepper and salt.
Stir in the flour and gradually add the stock and cider or
Guinness, stirring all the while. Bring to a boil and simmer
for fifteen minutes, stirring from time to time.

In the meantime, melt the remaining butter in a frying
pan and add the lamb cubes and garlic. Sauté for five minutes, turning frequently. Set aside until the vegetables are
ready. Check that the sauce is well seasoned and transfer to
a shallow serving dish. Put the lamb on top of the vegetables,
sprinkle with chopped parsley and serve. If you are serving
croutons, make them in triangles and place them around the
edge of the dish.

4 SERVINGS

Lamb Shrewsbury

This recipe, which comes from a very special friend, Rosemary Bett, is her version of a traditional British dish of the same name. It's not at all hard to prepare and the results are invariably delicious.

2 *pounds meat from the neck or shoulder of lamb, cut into small chunks, or 8 lamb cutlets*
3 *tablespoons vegetable oil*
1¼ *cups sliced mushrooms*
1 *tablespoon flour*
4 *tablespoons red currant jelly*

2 *teaspoons Worcestershire sauce*
Juice of one lemon
1 *cup beef stock*
Salt
Freshly ground black pepper
Pinch of nutmeg
3 *tablespoons chopped parsley*

Trim any fat off the lamb. Heat the oil in a large frying pan and brown the lamb on all sides. Transfer to a casserole and add the mushrooms.

Add the flour to the oil still in the frying pan. If necessary, add a little more oil to make a medium-thick paste. Stir for a few minutes until the flour turns golden brown, but do not let it brown. Add the red currant jelly, Worcestershire sauce and lemon juice. Continue to stir and add enough of the stock to make a thick gravy. Bring to a boil and season generously with salt, pepper and nutmeg.

Preheat oven to 325°.

Strain the gravy over the lamb and mushrooms. Cover the dish and cook in the oven for one and a half hours.

Sprinkle with parsley immediately before serving.

4 SERVINGS

Meat Pies

M eat pies are uniquely British. The very use of the term appears to have no foreign equivalent, and some etymologists believe it is derived from magpie, that notorious bird which pilfers and hoards stolen objects in his nest. They even make a connection between any collection of ingredients covered with a pastry crust and the nefarious contents of a magpie's nest.

The earliest pies on record are savoury, but gradually spices and dried fruits were added and, by the eighteenth century, pies were firmly divided into sweet and savoury. The latter were originally both lined and covered with pastry. However, in time the crust was most often used only to cover the pie and sometimes was even replaced by potatoes. Updating traditional pies and inventing new ones has become a popular pastime among British chefs and cooks and the recipes that follow can all be considered variations on a historical theme.

The pudding, like the pie, was originally a collection of savoury ingredients, but these were cooked in the stomach bag of an animal, commonly prepared by a butcher to use up his "bits and pieces." Later, a cloth took the place of a stomach bag and, in time, a suet crust and basin. Today, the term pudding is used for both savoury and sweet mixtures and, to confuse matters even more, has gone on to become synonomous with the word *dessert* in many English households.

Grasmere Lamb Pie

In the days when mutton was still mutton and true lamb could only be obtained in the spring, this recipe was a popular Cumbrian solution for cooking a fatty and tough leg of mutton. Today, a much streamlined version of this traditional dish regularly appears on the menu at Michael's Nook.

1 *leg of lamb,*
approximately 5 pounds
2 *tablespoons vegetable oil*
2 *tablespoons unsalted*
butter
3 *medium-sized onions,*
coarsely chopped
½ *cup flour*
⅔ *cup strong chicken stock*
1½ *cups red wine*
¾ *cup port*
¾ *cup raisins*
5 *dried apricots, coarsely*
chopped

5 *pitted prunes, coarsely*
chopped
2 *tablespoons red currant*
jelly
½ *teaspoon freshly ground*
black pepper
½ *teaspoon ground*
coriander
½ *teaspoon allspice*
½ *teaspoon cinnamon*
Salt
6 *ounces Shortcrust Pastry*
(see page 64)
1 *egg yolk, beaten with a*
little water

Preheat the oven to 300°.

Cut away the lamb from the bone, trim off any fat and cut the meat into one-inch cubes. Heat the oil in a frying pan, add the lamb and brown on all sides.

Meanwhile, heat the butter in a large flameproof and ovenproof casserole and lightly brown the onions. Add the browned lamb pieces to the casserole, stir in the flour and cook gently for about three minutes on top of the stove. Add the stock, wine and port and bring to a boil. Add the fruit, jelly and spices, season with salt and transfer the casserole, covered, to the oven. Cook for one and one-quarter hours.

Turn the oven temperature up to 400°. Transfer the meat and just enough juice to cover to a ten-inch round or oval pie dish. Roll out the pastry to fit the pie dish and place it over the meat. Press down the edges over the rim with a fork and make a few small gashes to allow the steam to escape. Brush with a little beaten egg yolk and bake in the oven until the pastry is golden (approximately 20 minutes).

6 TO 8 SERVINGS

Dartmouth Pie

Dartmoor, like Cumbria, is populated by huge numbers of sheep and, at the Carved Angel in Dartmouth, Joyce Molyneux serves her version of a local lamb pie. The Carved Angel is several hundred miles from Michael's Nook but it is interesting to see how similar a Dartmouth Pie is to the previous recipe.

2 pounds stewing lamb
 Salt
 Freshly ground black pepper
1 tablespoon flour
1 teaspoon mace
2 teaspoons cinnamon
2 teaspoons ground coriander
2 teaspoons peppercorns
2 tablespoons vegetable oil
3 medium-sized onions,
 finely chopped

2 cups beef stock
 Grated rind and juice of
 one orange
¾ cup pitted prunes
¾ cup dried apricots
⅔ cup raisins
6 ounces Shortcrust Pastry
 (see page 64)
1 egg yolk, beaten with a
 little water

Preheat the oven to 300°.

Trim the lamb, season it with a little salt and pepper and rub in the flour. Mix the spices together in a food processor or small mortar and sprinkle over the meat.

Heat the oil in a large frying pan and brown the meat.

Add the onions and cook for three minutes. Transfer the mixture to a large flameproof and ovenproof casserole. Add the stock, orange juice and rind and the dried fruit. Bring to a boil and season with a little more salt. Cover the dish and place in the oven for one and a half hours.

Take the casserole from the oven, remove the lid and allow to cool.

Raise oven temperature to 350°.

Roll out the pastry and place the meat mixture and all the liquid in individual pie dishes or in one ten-inch round or large oval dish. Cover with the pastry, press down the edges and make a few small gashes to allow the steam to escape. Use any remaining bits of pastry to decorate the middle of the pie. Brush the pastry top with the beaten egg yolk and bake in the oven until the pastry is golden (approximately 20 minutes).

6 TO 8 SERVINGS

Chicken Cider Pie

In medieval times, fowl were kept for laying eggs and producing chicks and not slaughtered until they got exceedingly scraggy and decrepit. Consequently, they were extremely tough and needed prolonged cooking in order to make them edible. For this reason they were most often used in soups, pies or puddings. Kentish chicken pudding, which is steamed for two hours in a suet pastry case, is one of the best known of the chicken puddings. My version is a pie made with shortcrust pastry that takes much less time to prepare and cook. The chicken is braised in cider and spiced with coriander and sage. This gives it an unusually sweet and spicy taste.

2 tablespoons vegetable oil
2 medium-sized onions,
 finely chopped
1½ pounds boned chicken
1 cup coarsely grated
 carrots
2 teaspoons ground
 coriander
1 teaspoon sage
2½ tablespoons flour
2 cups country cider

1 teaspoon French mustard
 Juice of one lemon
 Salt
 Freshly ground black
 pepper
2 cups sliced mushrooms
¼ cup heavy cream
6 ounces Shortcrust Pastry
 (see page 64)
1 egg yolk, beaten with a
 little water

Preheat the oven to 300°.

Heat the oil in a flameproof and ovenproof casserole and add the onions. Cut the chicken into cubes of about one inch and add to the onions. Allow the meat to brown on all sides over medium heat and then add the carrots, coriander and sage. Stir in the flour and cook for one minute before gradually pouring in the cider, stirring all the time, so that the sauce thickens without becoming lumpy. Add the mustard and lemon juice and season with salt and pepper.

Cover the casserole and transfer it to the oven. Cook for 30 minutes, add the mushrooms and cream and cook for another ten minutes—the sauce should now be thick and creamy. If it is runny, blend a little of the sauce with some additional flour and then stir it into the main sauce.

Allow to cool slightly and then transfer the mixture to a large Pyrex or ovenproof pie dish approximately ten inches in diameter.

Roll out the pastry to fit the pie dish and cover the chicken mixture. Press down the edges with a fork and make two small gashes in the pastry to allow the steam to escape. Cut the remaining pastry into small leaves and use them to decorate the center of the pie. Brush the pastry with the beaten egg yolk and bake in the oven for 25 to 30 minutes until the top of the pie is golden brown.

6 SERVINGS

Beefsteak, Kidney and Oyster Pudding

Who is not familiar with steak and kidney pudding—the pride of British cuisine—served in its own basin, neatly wrapped in a freshly laundered white napkin and accompanied by brussels sprouts and new potatoes? Much less familiar is the version of this pudding which contains oysters and has always been popular in the Midlands and north of England, and in Scotland is known as Musselburgh Pie. It may seem odd to mix oysters with meat but the combination works well and was extremely popular in Victorian England when oysters were plentiful and every town had its oyster stalls. Unfortunately, oysters were so popular that the British oyster beds have never recovered from the indiscriminate depletion of their stock, so oysters today are of course a high-priced delicacy.

3 *tablespoons vegetable oil*
1 *medium-sized onion,*
   chopped
1 *pound top round steak,*
   cut into one-inch cubes
½ *pound veal or beef kidneys,*
   cut into half-inch pieces
2 *tablespoons flour*
1 *cup thickly sliced*
   mushrooms
20 *oysters*
1 *bay leaf*
   Salt
   Freshly ground black
   pepper

2 *tablespoons Worcestershire*
   sauce
1 *cup beef stock*
½ *cup oyster juice*
1 *tablespoon tomato purée*

SUET PASTRY

2 *cups flour*
2 *teaspoons baking powder*
1 *cup shredded suet*
   Salt
   Freshly ground black
   pepper
6 *tablespoons cold water*

Place two tablespoons of the oil in a large frying pan and add the onion. Remove any fat or gristle from the steak cubes and kidneys and coat them with flour. Sauté in the oil until they are browned and then set aside, with the onion, in a mixing bowl. Add one tablespoon of oil to the frying pan and sauté the mushrooms for one minute. Add the mushrooms to the meat and then mix in the oysters, bay leaf, a liberal sprinkling of salt and pepper, the Worcestershire sauce, meat stock, oyster juice and the tomato purée. Set aside to cool to room temperature.

To prepare the pastry: Combine the flour, baking powder and suet in a bowl. Add a generous pinch of salt and a little pepper. Continue mixing until the mixture has the consistency of coarse breadcrumbs, then add the cold water, one tablespoon at a time. Mix to a soft dough, kneading as little as possible. If the dough is too crumbly, add a little more water, but don't make it too sticky as it should be on the dry side.

Form the dough into a ball and place it on a lightly floured surface. Cut off two-thirds and roll into a circle large enough to line a greased English pudding bowl or other bowl that holds approximately six cups and has a diameter of six and one-half inches. Work the dough around the sides so that it fits neatly and reaches just over the rim. Fill the basin with the cooled steak and oyster mixture and roll out the remaining pastry to cover the top. Fold over the edges of the dough lining the bowl. Moisten the edges with water so that they adhere well to the pastry top. Crimp down with a fork so that the dough is sealed very tightly, and trim off any excess pastry.

Take a piece of foil quite a bit larger than the diameter of the basin. Make a pleat in it, place over the pie, and tie it around the top of the basin—it should be slack in the middle so that the pastry can rise but secured tightly around the edge so that no steam or water can get in.

Place the basin on a steamer rack or an inverted saucer in a large saucepan and fill it halfway up with water. Cover the pan with a tight-fitting lid, bring to a boil and cook the pudding in gently boiling water for three hours. Check from time to time and top up the water to maintain the same level.

Remove the basin from the water. Untie the covering and tie a white napkin around the basin before serving.

6 SERVINGS

Leek and Veal Pasties

Pasties (the *a* pronounced as in *lass*) are individual meat pies. The best known of these turnovers is the Cornish pasty. However, Priddy Oggies, Tiddy Oggies and Lancashire Foot are all members of the pasty family. Many cooks today have their own particular favorites and although I am a great fan of the traditional Cornish pasty with its filling of beef, onions, potatoes and carrots, I also happen to like my own variation—Leek and Veal Pasties. Serve them either hot or at room temperature with a green salad.

12 *ounces Shortcrust Pastry (see page 64)*	*Salt*
¾ *pound veal fillet*	*Freshly ground black pepper*
3 *medium-sized leeks*	3 *tablespoons veal or chicken stock*
10 *coriander leaves (cilantro), chopped, or* ½ *teaspoon ground coriander*	¼ *cup chopped parsley*
½ *teaspoon chopped fresh thyme or* ¼ *teaspoon dried thyme*	1 *egg, lightly beaten*

Preheat the oven to 400°.

Roll out the pastry on a lightly floured surface until it is approximately one-eighth of an inch thick. Cut into five-inch rounds, using a plate or saucer to measure each round.

Trim away any skin or gristle from the veal and dice it into small cubes. Wash and trim the leeks, cut away the green leaves and chop the remaining white parts into small pieces. Mix together the meat, leeks, coriander, thyme, a generous amount of salt and pepper, the meat stock and the parsley. Place an equal amount of the mixture down the middle of each round in the shape of a little sausage. Brush the edges of the pastry with a little beaten egg and bring the sides up to meet in the center over the top of the filling so that each pasty looks like an oval-shaped mound. Pinch the edges tightly together, crimp or flute with a fork, and make two half-inch splits or vents on each side of the pasties so that the steam can escape while cooking. Brush the pasties with the remaining egg and place them seams up on a lightly greased cookie sheet. Bake for ten minutes, reduce the heat to 350° and bake for approximately 35 minutes or until the pasties are golden brown. Serve hot or at room temperature.

4 TO 6 SERVINGS

Vegetables

Finding fresh vegetables in England has never been difficult. The problem has been that they are often too large (English farmers love to grow huge vegetables, a habit hard to curb since the much-coveted ribbons at local flower and vegetable shows generally go to the largest entries.) But it is in the preparation that the real trouble lies. The English tend to overcook their vegetables. A fine, crisp, young carrot enters many a British kitchen only to emerge sad, wet and weary from the ordeal.

However, this has mercifully begun to change, and today it is probably by their vegetables more than anything that one can recognize the new breed of British chef and cook. New potatoes, tiny peas, young carrots and onions from which the vigor has not all been drained are more and more evident. At last they are allowed to be themselves again. Another welcome development is that root vegetables are coming back into favor and the long-neglected parsnip, turnip, rutabaga and Jerusalem artichoke are making an encouraging comeback. A wonderful cast of vegetables is in fact waiting in the wings.

Vegetables

Parsnip Purée
Parsnip Balls
Parsnips, Potatoes and
    Bacon
Crisp Fried Parsnips
Glazed Turnips
Steamed Vegetables with
    Horseradish and Dill
Lancashire Cheese and
    Onions

Beetroot Purée
Hot Beetroot with Garlic
Buttered Cabbage
Braised Cabbage with
    Juniper and Garlic
Turnip Colcannon
Rumpledethumps
New Potato and Radish
    Salad

Parsnip Purée

Parsnips make an excellent and unusual purée. For an interesting contrast in texture, try serving a parsnip purée with nuts. John Tovey of Miller Howe in the Lake District mixes his purée with two tablespoons of pine nuts; Ron Titley with pistachios. Both are good.

1½ *pounds parsnips*
    Salt
6 *tablespoons unsalted*
    butter

Juice of half a lemon
Freshly ground black pepper

Peel the parsnips and place in a pan of boiling salted water and cook for 20 minutes or until the parsnips are soft. Purée in a food processor or blender, add the butter and lemon juice and season to taste with salt and pepper.

6 SERVINGS

Parsnip Balls

The parsnip is a genuine, indigenous British vegetable, which even today grows wild in many parts of the countryside. It has been eaten since the earliest times and, long before the potato made its appearance, the parsnip was the accompaniment of choice for roast beef. It was also traditionally served with boiled salt cod on Ash Wednesday. These parsnip cakes are from an old recipe that I have adapted slightly. They are good with beef and lamb.

1 pound young parsnips
3 medium-sized potatoes
  Salt
½ cup heavy cream
 4 tablespoons unsalted
   butter
¼ teaspoon mace
¼ teaspoon nutmeg

2 tablespoons chopped
  parsley
  Freshly ground black
  pepper
  Flour
1 cup toasted breadcrumbs
  Vegetable oil

Peel the parsnips and the potatoes, cut them into small pieces and boil them in salted water until cooked. Mash them with a fork and add the cream and butter. Then mix in the mace, nutmeg and chopped parsley and season with salt and pepper.

The mixture will now be rather sticky. Dip your fingers in a little flour and shape the mixture into small balls—about one and a half inches in diameter. Roll each ball in breadcrumbs, cover and refrigerate for at least one hour.

Fry the balls in a little hot oil until they are crisp and golden on the outside. (If you prefer, they can be deep fried.) Serve immediately.

4 TO 6 SERVINGS

Parsnips, Potatoes and Bacon

This is an old country method for cooking parsnips to which I have added cheese. It is terribly simple to prepare and absolutely delicious.

1 *pound parsnips*
5 *medium-sized potatoes*
8 *slices bacon, chopped into*
  one-inch pieces

1 *cup chicken stock*
  Salt
  Freshly ground black
  pepper
½ *cup grated Cheddar cheese*

Preheat the oven to 350°.

Peel the parsnips and the potatoes and cut them into two-inch strips. Mix them with the bacon and place in a well-greased ovenproof dish. Pour in the stock and sprinkle with a generous amount of salt and pepper. Cover and bake in the oven for 45 minutes. Remove the cover and sprinkle the cheese over the top. Cook uncovered for an additional ten minutes.

4 TO 6 SERVINGS

Crisp Fried Parsnips

Here is another way to prepare parsnips that is rather similar to making a rosti. It's very simple to do and quite delicious.

1 *pound parsnips*
  Salt

4 *tablespoons unsalted butter*
  Freshly ground black pepper

Peel and cut the parsnips into thin sticks about two inches long. Drop them into a saucepan of boiling salted water and

cook until almost tender (three or four minutes). Drain and
pat them dry with paper towels.

Melt the butter in a large frying pan and add the parsnips. Fry over medium heat until they are brown and crisp.
Season to taste with salt and pepper and serve immediately.

4 TO 6 SERVINGS

Glazed Turnips

I used to be suspicious of turnips—bad school memories I
suppose—but not any more. This particular recipe had a lot
to do with my conversion.

1 *pound turnips (the*
smallest possible)
Salt
2 *tablespoons unsalted butter*

3 *tablespoons brown sugar*
Freshly ground black pepper
2 *tablespoons chopped parsley*

Wash and clean the turnips. Trim off both ends and cut them
into quarters. Place them in a saucepan of boiling salted
water and cook until they are almost tender (about ten minutes). Drain and set aside.

In a separate saucepan, melt the butter. Add the sugar
and when it has melted, add the turnips. Cook, uncovered,
over low heat until the turnips are glazed with the butter-
sugar syrup. Season to taste with salt and pepper and sprinkle
the parsley on top before serving.

4 SERVINGS

Steamed Vegetables with Horseradish and Dill

Horseradish is too good to use only with cold meat. It can be used to great effect with vegetables as well. This recipe is a godsend for those dreadful winter days when no vegetable in the shop looks good enough to be eaten straight. However, it cannot be prepared ahead of time or the vegetables will become mushy and lose all their texture.

1 *pound brussels sprouts, as small as possible*
1½ *pounds small red potatoes, cut into half-inch slices*
3 *leeks, washed, trimmed and cut into half-inch slices*
3 *medium-sized carrots, cut into thin strips two inches in length*

Salt
6 *tablespoons unsalted butter*
3 *tablespoons freshly grated horseradish*
3 *tablespoons cider vinegar*
1 *bunch fresh dill, finely chopped*
Freshly ground black pepper

Trim any coarse outer leaves from the brussels sprouts and score them with crosses on the bottom. Place the sprouts, unpeeled potatoes, leeks and carrots in a vegetable steamer, sprinkle with salt, and steam, covered, for approximately twelve minutes or until the vegetables are tender but still firm.

While the vegetables are steaming, heat the butter in a heavy saucepan and stir in the horseradish, vinegar and dill. Add a little salt and pepper and then toss the vegetables in the sauce. Serve immediately.

6 SERVINGS

Lancashire Cheese and Onions

An old Lancashire dish that has been updated by Jean Butterworth and appears regularly on her menu at White Moss House, a small but very comfortable hotel in Grasmere, overlooking Rydal Water. The hotel, which has only seven rooms, started out as a bed and breakfast several years ago. However, once the guests began to sample Jean Butterworth's cooking, dinner at White Moss House became the focal point of an overnight stay. Mrs. Butterworth, who grew up in Lancashire, is now helped in the kitchen by her son-in-law. Every night they provide a set four-course meal with no choice except for dessert. Mrs. Butterworth tells me that this dish is always a favorite with her guests, many of whom return year after year.

6 *medium-sized onions,*
coarsely chopped
Salt
½ *cup plus 2 tablespoons*
milk
1½ *teaspoons cornstarch*
1½ *cups grated Lancashire*

cheese (or any good
melting cheese)
1½ *cups grated Lancashire*
Salt
Freshly ground black
pepper
Freshly grated nutmeg

Preheat oven to 300°.

Place the onions in a casserole, sprinkle them with salt and add one cup of water. Cover the casserole and bake in the oven until the onions are soft but not colored (about 20 minutes).

Mix the milk with the cornstarch in a saucepan over gentle heat until smooth and then pour the mixture over the onions. Sprinkle with grated cheese. Return the casserole to the oven and continue to cook until the cheese has melted (about ten minutes). Season to taste with salt and pepper and sprinkle some grated nutmeg on top of the dish before serving.

4 SERVINGS

Beetroot Purée

Beetroot, English for beets, is not received with any great enthusiasm in most quarters either here or there. Disdain and disparagement seem to be the usual reactions. However, this vegetable does not deserve its poor reputation. Not only is it possessed of a glorious color but as long as beets are small, they taste delicious. This purée is a case in point.

1 *pound fresh beets*
2 *carrots, chopped*
 Salt
4 *tablespoons unsalted butter,*
 cut into small pieces

½ *cup heavy cream*
 Freshly ground black
 pepper

Wash the beets and remove their stalks. Drop them into a saucepan of boiling salted water and cook until tender (about 25 minutes, depending on size and age). To determine whether a beet is cooked, press it gently with your fingers. If the skin starts to come off, it is done. After cooking them for fifteen minutes add the carrots.

Allow the beets to cool a little and then peel off the skins. Purée the beets and carrots with the butter and cream in a food processor or blender. Return the purée to a clean saucepan and season to taste with salt and pepper. Reheat gently until the purée is hot and serve.

4 TO 6 SERVINGS

Hot Beetroot with Garlic

Another unusual method guaranteed to overcome any preconceptions about this neglected vegetable.

1 *pound fresh beets*
 Salt
4 *tablespoons unsalted butter*
2 *cloves garlic, finely chopped*
1 *medium-sized onion, finely chopped*

Grated rind of half an orange
2 *tablespoons orange juice*
 Freshly ground black pepper

Wash the beets and remove their stalks. Drop them into a saucepan of boiling salted water and cook until tender (about 25 minutes, depending on size and age). To determine whether a beet is cooked, press it gently with your fingers. If the skin starts to come off easily, it is done. Allow the beets to cool and then peel off the skins.

Melt the butter in a large saucepan, add the garlic and onion and cook over medium heat until soft. Dice the beets and add them to the pan, together with the orange rind and orange juice. Cook for one minute and season to taste with salt and pepper.

4 TO 6 SERVINGS

Buttered Cabbage

Dreadfully maligned and the butt of endless jokes, cabbage has come to symbolize all that is bad about British cooking. Actually, it has never been a particularly popular vegetable in Britain—both Mrs. Acton and Mrs. Beeton give their readers only one method for cooking cabbage in contrast to their many recipes for other vegetables. Perhaps they are in part responsible for its reputation for monotony. In fact, when not overcooked, cabbage has a delicate and wonderful taste, but retaining some of the original crispness is essential.

1 *medium-sized cabbage*   4 *tablespoons unsalted butter*
   (*about 2 pounds*), *cored*   1 *teaspoon lemon juice*
   and cut into fine strips   *Freshly ground black pepper*
   Salt

Place the cabbage in a vegetable steamer set in a pan of salted water. Sprinkle some salt over the cabbage, bring to a boil, cover and boil until the cabbage is still crisp but starting to get tender (about three minutes). Drain in a colander under cold water and press out any remaining water.

Melt the butter in a saucepan, add the cabbage and lemon juice and season to taste with salt and pepper. Stir for two minutes or until the butter is absorbed into the cabbage. Serve immediately.

4 TO 6 SERVINGS

Braised Cabbage with Juniper and Garlic

This is another recipe from Murdo MacSween, whose Aunt Chrissie, the wife of Sir Compton MacKenzie, first taught him to cook. The addition of junipers and garlic gives the cabbage an unusually piquant flavor.

2 *tablespoons unsalted butter*
1 *medium-sized cabbage*
   (*about 2 pounds*), *cored*
   and cut into fine strips
2 *small onions, finely chopped*
   Salt

Pinch of nutmeg
2 *cloves garlic, crushed*
12 *juniper berries, crushed*
½ *cup chicken stock*
   Freshly ground black
   pepper

Preheat the oven to 300°.

Melt the butter in a flameproof and ovenproof dish and add the cabbage and onion. Sprinkle with salt and sauté for five minutes. Add the nutmeg, garlic and crushed juniper berries. Pour in the stock and bake in the oven for 20 minutes. Season to taste with salt and pepper.

4 TO 6 SERVINGS

Turnip Colcannon

Colcannon, from *kailcannon*, is the Irish version of Bubble and Squeak and is traditionally served at Halloween. Bubble and Squeak gets its name from the sounds made when the cooked cabbage and the potatoes are fried together in hot oil. Colcannon, on the other hand, is made with mashed potatoes; the *Oxford Dictionary* suggests that the root of the word is from *kale* (cabbage) and *cannon*, as at one time the vegetables used were first pounded with a cannon ball. Turnip Colcannon is a variation I particularly like as the addition of the turnips gives the dish an unusual flavor.

5 potatoes, peeled and
  halved
7 medium-sized turnips,
  peeled and quartered
1 teaspoon salt
½ cup milk

6 tablespoons unsalted butter
2 cups coarsely chopped
  cabbage
2 teaspoons wine vinegar
Salt
Freshly ground black
  pepper

In a large saucepan, cover the potatoes with cold water. Bring to a boil and add the turnips and the salt. Simmer for 30 minutes or until the vegetables are tender. Drain and purée with a potato masher or through a food mill. Return them to the saucepan and stir in the milk and four tablespoons of butter.

Steam the cabbage for five minutes and then toss it with the vinegar. Beat into the purée, add salt and pepper and top with the remaining butter. Serve immediately.

6 SERVINGS

Rumpledethumps

Here is another version of Colcannon where leeks are added to the potatoes and the cabbage. Though this dish can hardly be classified as *nouvelle Anglaise,* it is delicious.

5 potatoes, peeled and cut in
   half
   Salt
5 cups shredded cabbage
2 leeks, washed, trimmed
   and sliced

¾ cup milk
8 tablespoons unsalted butter
   Freshly ground black
   pepper
¼ teaspoon mace
1 cup grated Cheddar cheese

Boil the potatoes in salted water for fifteen minutes or until they are cooked. In a separate saucepan, bring two cups of salted water to a boil and cook the cabbage and leeks for five minutes. Drain and set aside.

Drain the potatoes and mash them in a large bowl. Stir in the milk and half the butter. Add the cabbage and leeks and season to taste with salt and pepper. Stir in the mace and place the mixture in a buttered ovenproof casserole.

Melt the remaining butter and dribble it over the potato mixture. Sprinkle the cheese on top and place under the broiler for three to four minutes.

4 TO 6 SERVINGS

New Potato and Radish Salad

A delicious and unusual potato salad that is nice on picnics.

1 *pound small red potatoes,*
  scrubbed
8 *small radishes, thinly sliced*
2 *tablespoons chopped fresh*
  mint

2 *tablespoons white wine*
  vinegar
½ *teaspoon salt*
  Freshly ground black
  pepper
⅛ *teaspoon sugar*
⅓ *cup olive oil*

Boil the unpeeled potatoes until tender, about fifteen minutes. Cut into quarters. Place them in a serving bowl and toss with the radishes and mint.

Whisk the vinegar with the salt, some pepper and the sugar. Slowly beat in the oil. Pour the vinaigrette over the vegetables. Allow to cool before serving.

4 TO 6 SERVINGS

Sauces and
Dressings

Sauces, whatever the pundits might say, have played an important role in British cooking for centuries. And the British taste for piquant sauces, particularly those made from fruits, appears to have been greater even than in the rest of Europe. Gooseberry sauce served with mackerel was a Norman specialty. Fruit may have been favored partly due to the fact that the white flour needed for most other kinds of sauces was a great luxury in Britain during the Middle Ages.

Some of the best-known British sauces such as Cumberland, mint, bread and Madeira are not included in this chapter. I didn't want to plagiarize my earlier book, *Great British Cooking: A Well-Kept Secret*, where they can all be found. Instead, here is a selection of some sauces that are lesser known and some that are variations of traditional ones.

Sauces and Dressings

Savoury Sauces

Green Pepper Sauce
Simple Parsley Sauce
Herb and Cream Sauce
Cucumber Sauce
Cucumber and Horseradish
    Sauce
Tomato and Horseradish
    Sauce
Mustard and Dill Sauce

Mustard Butter Sauce
Ritz Cranberry Sauce
Spiced Cranberries
Brandied Purée of Apples
    and Onions
Onion Marmalade
Sweet Onion and Mint
    Purée
Fresh Basil Jelly

Sweet Sauces

Coffee Sauce

Orange Custard

Savoury Sauces

Green Pepper Sauce

This recipe comes from Richard Sandford, who serves it with his Marinated Duck (see page 95), and it is a delicious sauce with any kind of poultry or game.

5 *tablespoons unsalted butter*	½ *cup brandy*
1 *small onion, finely chopped,*	2 *teaspoons green*
or 2 shallots, chopped	*peppercorns*
1 *cup chicken stock*	⅓ *cup heavy cream*

Place one tablespoon of the butter in a saucepan and melt over gentle heat. Add the onion or the shallots and sauté for two minutes. Pour in the stock and boil rapidly until the liquid has reduced to half the original amount. Add the brandy and boil for another two minutes.

Remove the saucepan from the heat and beat in the remaining butter cut into small pieces. Add the peppercorns and cream and heat without bringing again to a boil.

1 CUP

Simple Parsley Sauce

Parsley sauce is traditionally served with fish, especially smoked haddock. However, it is not often prepared with a fish stock base as in the case of this recipe, which comes from Chewton Glen, where it is served with a Fish Choucroute (see page 78).

1½ cups fish stock
½ cup white wine
2 shallots, finely chopped
1 bunch parsley
2 cups heavy cream

2 tablespoons unsalted butter
Salt
Freshly ground black pepper

Heat the fish stock, wine, shallots and parsley stalks slowly in a heavy-bottomed pan. Simmer until the mixture has reduced to half its original amount. During this time, blanch the parsley leaves by placing them in a saucepan of cold water, bringing to a boil and simmering for one minute. Drain and set aside.

Add the cream to the reduced stock. Return to a simmer and cook until the sauce thickens. Strain and blend in a food processor or blender with the blanched parsley leaves. Return the sauce to the saucepan. Add the butter in pieces, stir until smooth and season to taste with salt and pepper.

2 CUPS

Herb and Cream Sauce

This is a simple white sauce to which is added a little mustard and several herbs. Use fresh herbs if possible as the difference is remarkable. It is a sauce served at the Carved Angel by Joyce Molyneux with her Salmon in Pastry with Ginger and Currants (see page 63) but it is also delicious with any freshwater fish.

2 tablespoons unsalted butter
2 shallots, finely chopped
2 tablespoons chopped parsley
1 tablespoon chopped fresh
 chervil or 1 teaspoon
 dried chervil
1 tablespoon fresh tarragon
 or 1 teaspoon dried tarragon

1 teaspoon flour
1¼ cups heavy cream
1 teaspoon coarse-grained
 mustard
1 egg yolk, beaten
½ teaspoon lemon juice
Salt
Freshly ground black
 pepper

Melt the butter in a small saucepan over gentle heat and add the shallots. Sauté them in the butter for a few minutes and add the herbs. Cook a minute or two longer.

Add the flour, mixing well, and then the cream. Bring gently to a boil, stirring well with a wooden spoon. Cook for about five minutes.

Add the mustard, the egg yolk and the lemon juice. Season to taste with salt and pepper.

1½ CUPS

Cucumber Sauce

Anthony Pitt of Homewood Park serves Cucumber Sauce with his Salmon and Dill Fishcakes (see page 66). One of the easiest sauces of all to prepare, it is excellent not only with most fish but also as a condiment with curry. It could even be called the British version of raita!

1 *medium-sized cucumber*	2 *tablespoons chopped fresh*
2¼ *cups yogurt*	*mint*
	½ *clove garlic, crushed*

Peel the cucumber, remove the seeds and chop into very small cubes. Mix together with all the other ingredients and chill before serving.

3 CUPS

Cucumber and Horseradish Sauce

This and the following recipe are two variations on a well-established favorite.

1 *cucumber, peeled and*	3 *tablespoons freshly grated*
finely diced	*horseradish or* ¼ *cup*
Salt	*bottled white horseradish,*
Freshly ground black pepper	*drained and squeezed dry*
2 *tablespoons tarragon*	½ *teaspoon sugar*
vinegar	
1 *cup sour cream or* 1 *cup*	
heavy cream, beaten stiff	

Sprinkle the cucumber with a little salt and pepper, place it in a dish and sprinkle the vinegar over the top. Leave for fifteen minutes.

Place the cream in a bowl, drain the cucumber and stir in, together with the horseradish and the sugar. Cover and refrigerate until ready to serve.

2 CUPS

Tomato and Horseradish Sauce

3 tablespoons freshly grated
  horseradish or 1/4 cup
  bottled white horseradish,
  drained and squeezed dry
1 teaspoon lemon juice
1/2 teaspoon sugar ·
1/4 teaspoon prepared English
  mustard

1 cup sour cream or 1 cup
  heavy cream, beaten stiff
2 medium-sized tomatoes,
  peeled and diced
Salt

Mix the horseradish, lemon juice, sugar and mustard in a small bowl. Fold in the cream and tomatoes. Stir in a pinch of salt. Cover and refrigerate until ready to serve.

2 CUPS

Mustard and Dill Sauce

I am devoted to English mustard and enjoy thinking of new ways to use it. This recipe and the one that follow are two of my more successful experiments. This is a cold sauce that is good with hot or cold ham and other cold meats.

¼ cup prepared English
   mustard
1 tablespoon sugar
3 tablespoons white wine
   vinegar

½ cup olive oil
4 tablespoons sour cream
4 tablespoons chopped fresh
   dill

Whisk together in a bowl the mustard, sugar and vinegar. Gradually beat in the oil. Fold in the sour cream and the dill. Cover and refrigerate.

½ CUP

Mustard Butter Sauce

Excellent with any kind of fish.

8 tablespoons unsalted butter
2 teaspoons prepared English
   mustard

1 teaspoon fresh lemon juice
Pinch of ground white
   pepper

Melt the butter over low heat in a saucepan and simmer gently for five minutes without browning. Remove from the heat and beat in the mustard gradually. When it is fully absorbed into the butter, add the lemon juice and the pepper.

½ CUP

Ritz Cranberry Sauce

Americans tend to have proprietary feelings about the cranberry. I have found there is often a certain lack of interest sometimes even verging on hostility when I point out that it is a berry that originally came from the fens around Cambridge and was imported to America by the first settlers. Be that as it may, this cranberry sauce, often served by Michael Quinn when at the Ritz, is a decidedly un-American version containing such ingredients as port and yogurt.

6 *tablespoons sugar*	½ *teaspoon cinnamon*
½ *cup port*	*Grated rind of one orange*
1 *pound fresh cranberries*	2 *teaspoons yogurt*
6 *tablespoons orange juice*	

In a deep pan, bring the sugar, port and a half cup of water to a rolling boil and reduce to half the original amount. In a separate pan, bring the cranberries and the orange juice to a boil. Cover and steam for approximately five minutes.

Remove the berries from their cooking liquor and add this liquor to the sugar and port. Return to a boil and add the cinnamon. Stir in the cranberries and simmer for five minutes. Remove from the heat and add the grated orange rind. Allow to cool and add the yogurt.

2 CUPS

Spiced Cranberries

This is another somewhat unusual use for cranberries. I once bought a jar of spiced cranberries at a village fête; they were marvelous with cold turkey. The following recipe is my best effort at re-creating this delicacy.

2½ *cups fresh cranberries*
  ½ *teaspoon grated fresh*
     ginger
  ½ *teaspoon allspice*
  2 *cinnamon sticks*

6 *cloves*
1 *cup cider vinegar*
1 *cup dark brown sugar*

Place the cranberries in a large saucepan. Add the spices and vinegar. Simmer until the cranberries are soft (about ten minutes). Add the sugar and bring to a boil. Simmer for 20 minutes. Remove the cinnamon sticks and pour into pots. Seal and refrigerate.

3 CUPS

Brandied Purée of Apples and Onions

What could be more traditional than applesauce with pork, and what could be more dull? Here is a rather more sophisticated variation. It goes well with pork and provides a welcome change for even the most conservative palate.

2 *medium-sized onions, finely chopped*	½ *cup white wine*
6 *tablespoons unsalted butter*	1 *cup brandy*
4 *Granny Smith apples, peeled, cored and sliced*	1 *cup heavy cream*
	Salt
	Ground white pepper

Sauté the onions in four tablespoons of butter in a heavy-bottomed saucepan until they are soft and golden. Add the apples, wine and half the brandy. Cover and simmer for 20 minutes.

Purée the mixture in a food processor or blender. Return to the saucepan and bring to a simmer. Add the cream and continue to cook for five minutes. Add the remaining brandy and butter. Season to taste with salt and pepper. Serve at room temperature.

2 CUPS

Onion Marmalade

This is almost a chutney and can be served with cold meat, pâté or a terrine. The recipe comes from Homewood Park.

10 *medium-sized onions,*
   finely chopped
12 *tablespoons unsalted*
   butter
1¼ *cups sugar*
¼ *cup wine vinegar*

¼ *cup Madeira*
2¼ *cups red wine*
3 *teaspoons salt*
3 *teaspoons freshly ground*
   black pepper

Sauté the onions in the butter in a large heavy-bottomed saucepan until soft. Add the remaining ingredients and cook at a gentle simmer for one hour. Pour into jars or pots, seal and refrigerate.

3 CUPS

Sweet Onion and Mint Purée

British cooks frequently serve an onion sauce with lamb or goose but mint sauce is, of course, considered the appropriate accompaniment for roast lamb. In this recipe, I have combined both onions and mint. The result is hardly traditional but it is excellent with roast lamb and also good with rabbit.

6 *large red onions, finely*
   chopped
8 *tablespoons unsalted*
   butter
2¼ *cups milk*

3 *teaspoons chopped fresh*
   mint
Salt
Freshly ground black
pepper

Sauté the onions in the butter until soft. Add the milk and

mint and season to taste with salt and pepper. Simmer for ten minutes. Purée in a blender or a food processor. Check the seasoning and serve warm.

2 CUPS

Fresh Basil Jelly

Pesto has become so common today that it is in danger of giving basil itself that aura of too-great familiarity. It should be outlawed, wonderful as it is, for a decade or so, and we should turn at the same time to some of the other great occasions for using basil. Basil jelly is a case in point. Few people know how good it can be as an alternative to mint jelly.

½ cup tarragon vinegar
    Juice of one lemon
3 cups fresh basil leaves,
    picked over and washed
3 cups sugar

3 medium-sized green
    apples, cored and coarsely
    chopped
¼ cup liquid pectin
    Green food coloring
    (optional)

Place the vinegar, one and one-half cups of water and the lemon juice in a large enamel saucepan. Bring to a boil and boil for five minutes. Remove from the heat and add the basil leaves. Allow them to infuse for about ten minutes. Add the sugar and the apples. Bring to a rolling boil and when the sugar is dissolved, add the pectin and, if you wish, two or three drops of food coloring. Boil for one minute, strain through a fine sieve and pour the jelly into sterilized jelly glasses. Clean the tops and seal them.

4 HALF-PINT JELLY GLASSES

Sweet Sauces

Coffee Sauce

At Gravetye Manor, this sauce is served with a very rich Chocolate Whiskey Cake (see page 218). However, it is also excellent with ice cream.

4 egg yolks
2 tablespoons sugar
2 teaspoons coffee liqueur

1 cup milk
¼ cup heavy cream

Beat the egg yolks, sugar and coffee liqueur in a bowl. Warm the milk and pour it over the egg yolks, stirring all the time. Place the bowl over a saucepan filled with hot water or in the top of a double boiler and cook over gentle heat until the sauce thickens.

Allow the sauce to cool. Beat the cream until it is stiff and fold into the sauce.

1¼ CUPS

Orange Custard

Here is a variation on that most British of sauces, or should one say institutions—custard. Made from scratch, warm custard, perfectly smooth in texture, is to my mind quite heavenly. This recipe is a way to dress it up for more formal occasions.

1½ cups half-and-half
  1 vanilla bean or ½
    teaspoon vanilla extract
  3 long strips orange peel

5 egg yolks
½ cup sugar
3 tablespoons Cointreau

In a saucepan combine the half-and-half, vanilla bean, split in half, or vanilla extract and orange peel. Bring the mixture to a boil and remove the pan from the heat. Allow to cool for fifteen minutes.

Remove the orange peel and vanilla bean if used from the half-and-half. Beat the egg yolks until they are light and fluffy in a separate bowl and add the sugar slowly, beating until the mixture begins to form a ribbon. Then add the half-and-half, stirring while you pour it in. Transfer to a saucepan and cook over low heat, stirring until it thickens. Do not allow the mixture to boil. Remove from the heat and stir in the liqueur. Strain the custard into a jug or bowl. Cover with waxed paper and allow to chill for at least half an hour, unless serving hot.

2 CUPS

Puddings
(Desserts)

Strange as it may seem, the British call dessert of any sort pudding. And it is puddings that constitute, to my mind, the high point of British cooking. The proverbial English sweet tooth is almost a national characteristic and the word *sweet* is even used to mean pudding, so it is hardly surprising that there should be such an immense variety of British puddings.

Nowhere is the resurgence of interest in food and cooking more immediately evident than in the variations, re-creations and inventions of new and delicious ways to end a meal. Menus today proclaim a glorious profusion of tarts, syllabubs, steamed puddings, trifles, creams and flummeries. Rich, fattening and delicious, they are as much today as ever the pride of the British kitchen.

Where individual ramekins are called for in a recipe, use any medium-sized ramekins; I use ones that are one and one-half inches wide and three inches deep.

Puddings (Desserts)

Apple Charlotte
Baked Rum Apples
Priory Apple Tarts
Apple Tart with Cheddar
  Cheese
Apple Tart with Calvados,
  Brown Sugar and
  Tarragon
Special Apple Tart
Glazed Prune Tart
Old-Fashioned Curd Tart
Cumberland Rum Nicky
Westmorland Raisin and
  Nut Pie
Apricot Bakewell Tart
Almond Fruit Tart
Ipswich Almond Pudding
Duke of Cambridge Tart
Eighteenth-Century Lemon
  Cheesecake
Lemon and Almond Tart
Sticky Toffee Pudding
Butterscotch Cream Pie
Lemon Sponge Pudding
Marmalade Pudding
Treacle Pudding
Christopher Oakes's Bread
  and Butter Pudding
Baked Pear Pudding

Rhubarb Pudding
Rhubarb in a Honey and
  Saffron Custard
Peasant Girl with Veil
Tipsy Cake
Frozen Trifle
Blackberry and Red
  Currant Fool
Lemon Mousse
Chilled Mint and Chocolate
  Soufflé
Burnt Cream à l'Orange
Stone Cream
Flummery
Gooseberry and Orange
  Tansy
Peaches with Lemon and
  Brandy
Minted Strawberries
Strawberry Mille-Feuilles
Old English Syllabub
Orange Syllabub
Port Syllabub
Raspberry and Claret Jelly
Brown Bread Ice Cream
Gooseberry Ice Cream
Pistachio Ice Cream
Marzipan
Mint Sorbet

Apple Charlotte

Apple Charlotte was most likely named for Charlotte of Mecklenburg-Strelitz, queen consort of George III, who bore him fifteen children and, when he was declared insane in 1810, was more than ever in charge of the royal household. This dish which has immortalized her was originally made of apple marmalade covered in breadcrumbs. Today, it most often is given a pastry crust and uses apples themselves rather than marmalade. Half apples and half blackberries is another excellent variation (and frozen blackberries work perfectly well). The dish is sometimes called Apple Brown Betty. Serve warm with whipped cream or with Orange Custard (see page 155).

4 *large green apples* (*preferably Granny Smiths*)	1 *teaspoon lemon juice*
	½ *cup raisins*
	7 *slices good white bread,*
¼ *teaspoon cinnamon*	*buttered and with the*
6 *tablespoons unsalted butter*	*crusts removed*
4 *tablespoons orange marmalade*	½ *cup brown sugar*

Preheat the oven to 350°.

Peel, quarter and core the apples, then cut each quarter into three long segments. Place them, together with the cinnamon and the butter, in a saucepan. Heat gently and when the butter has melted and coated the apple slices, add the marmalade, lemon juice and raisins. Cook for five minutes over gentle heat and set aside.

Fit all but two slices of the bread in a buttered medium-sized (about five-cup) mold or pudding basin with the buttered sides facing out. Make sure that they fit together well and that there are no gaps. If necessary, trim the slices to improve the fit. Fill with the apple mixture and sprinkle the brown sugar over the top. Cover with the two remaining slices of bread, buttered sides up.

Place the mold in the oven and bake for 20 minutes. Reduce the oven temperature to 300° and bake for another 20 minutes. Remove the mold from the oven and allow to stand for ten minutes before turning the pudding out of the mold.

4 TO 6 SERVINGS

Baked Rum Apples

If one lives in a city, it is often difficult to find apples that have any taste. In these baked apples, the addition of rum, apricots and prunes helps disguise this deficiency, and produces a dish that is really quite special. Serve hot or cold with whipped cream.

6 *large tart, firm apples*   *Juice of half an orange*
   (*Mountain Spy are good*)   ¼ *cup dark brown sugar*
¼ *cup dried apricots*   1 *teaspoon allspice*
¼ *cup pitted prunes*   2 *tablespoons unsalted butter*
1 *cup rum*

Preheat the oven to 300°.

Core each apple and at the same time make a good-sized cavity in each. Chop the apricots and prunes into small pieces and stuff them into the cavities. Place the apples in a baking pan.

Mix the rum and orange juice and pour the mixture over the apples. Press down a small amount of brown sugar on top of each apple. Sprinkle some allspice on top and cover with a dab of butter.

Cover each apple with a small piece of foil and bake them for 50 minutes.

6 SERVINGS

Priory Apple Tarts

The next four recipes are for apple tarts but they are apple tarts with a difference. Three contain Calvados and all are fancy enough to serve on very special occasions. The first of these recipes comes from the Priory Hotel in Bath and consists of individual puff pastry apple tarts that are glazed under the broiler at the last moment. At the Priory, each tart is served surrounded by a raspberry sauce, which lends an extra festive note.

5 *large green cooking apples*	2 *tablespoons Calvados*
4 *tablespoons unsalted butter*	12 *ounces Puff Pastry*
4 *egg yolks*	(*see page 46*)
4 *tablespoons sugar*	6 *tablespoons apricot jam*

Preheat the oven to 350°.

Peel and core the apples, cut them into quarters and then slice them into segments one-eighth of an inch thick. Lay the apple slices on a cookie sheet that has been covered with waxed paper. Melt the butter and brush it over the apples. Place the cookie sheet in the oven for four minutes and then take it out. (This step will prevent the apples from discoloring.) Raise the oven temperature to 400°.

Beat the egg yolks, sugar and Calvados in a double boiler over gentle heat. Stir until the sauce thickens and then remove from the heat.

Roll out the pastry and use a five-and-a-half-inch diameter saucer or pastry ring to cut out six pastry rounds. Place the rounds on a greased cookie sheet and spread a layer of apricot jam on each of them. Lay the apple slices symmetrically on top of the apricot jam, leaving a small gap in the center. Place the tarts in the oven for ten minutes and then reduce the heat to 350°. Bake for another ten minutes or until the edge of the tarts and the apples are a pale golden color.

Place a spoonful of the sauce in the center of each tart and glaze under the broiler for a few seconds before serving.

6 SERVINGS

Apple Tart with Cheddar Cheese

It's a well-known fact that cheese goes well with apple pie but only Francis Coulson of Sharrow Bay Hotel would have thought to incorporate the cheese into the pastry itself.

PASTRY

2 cups flour
Pinch of salt
10 tablespoons unsalted butter, cut into small pieces
1¼ cups grated Cheddar cheese
1 egg yolk

FILLING

4 green cooking apples

2 tablespoons light brown sugar
1 tablespoon cornstarch
¼ teaspoon cinnamon
Pinch of nutmeg
4 tablespoons unsalted butter
2 tablespoons lemon juice
1 egg, beaten with a little water

Sift the flour and salt into a mixing bowl. Mix in the butter with your fingertips until the mixture resembles fine breadcrumbs. Mix in the cheese and then add the egg yolk. Mix with a knife until dough begins to form. Add a little water if the dough is too dry. Knead lightly until the pastry is smooth and has no cracks. Wrap it in waxed paper and refrigerate for 30 minutes.

Peel, core and slice the apples. Toss them in a plastic bag with the sugar, cornstarch, cinnamon and nutmeg.

Preheat the oven to 350°.

Roll out the pastry and use it to line a nine- or ten-inch pie pan. Place the apples in concentric circles, sprinkle with any sugar left in the bag and dot with pieces of butter. Sprinkle the lemon juice over the top. Use the remaining pastry to make thin strips, place them in lattice strips over the pie and brush the pastry with the beaten egg.

Bake in the oven until the pastry is golden brown (approximately 25 minutes).

6 SERVINGS

Apple Tart with Calvados, Brown Sugar and Tarragon

This delicious tart presents slices of apple lying on a purée of apples and fresh tarragon and covered with a syrup of Calvados and brown sugar in a case of puff pastry. Fresh tarragon is essential for this tart, so do not attempt it with dried tarragon. Serve either hot or cold with lots of whipped cream.

This is yet another recipe from the Castle Hotel in Taunton, which, under the extremely vigilant eye of its owner and manager, Kit Chapman, has become an outstanding example of the best kind of country hotel: one that offers comfort, good service (the staff is mostly young and exceptionally pleasant), excellent food and an outstanding wine list.

6 *ounces Puff Pastry*	7 *tablespoons brown sugar*
(*see page 46*)	1 *cup fresh tarragon*
5 *apples* (*preferably Granny*	4 *tablespoons unsalted butter*
Smiths)	¼ *cup Calvados*

Roll out the pastry to about one-eighth of an inch thick and use it to line a nine-inch flan ring. Refrigerate until ready to use.

Peel and core the apples and cut three of them into small slices. Place them, together with half the sugar and all the tarragon except for two leaves in a saucepan. Cook over gentle heat until you have a purée. If it seems too thick, add a little water. (I usually find I need about three tablespoons although it does depend on the juiciness of the apples.) Remove the saucepan from the heat and set aside.

Cut the two remaining apples into quarters and cut each quarter into three or four long segments. Melt the butter, the remaining sugar and the Calvados in a saucepan over gentle heat. Add the apple segments and glaze them in the sauce.

Preheat the oven to 375°.

Spoon the apple and tarragon purée over the pastry and then arrange the glazed apples on top in concentric circles. Pour any remaining Calvados sauce over the top.

Place the tart in the oven and bake for approximately 25 minutes or until the tart is golden brown.

4 TO 6 SERVINGS

Special Apple Tart

This recipe was given to me by a friend in Sussex. The apples are first soaked in the Calvados and then cooked in an open-faced tart in a custard that is also flavored with Calvados.

4 *green cooking apples*
¾ *cup Calvados*
6 *ounces Shortcrust Pastry*
  (see page 64)
3 *egg yolks*

5 *tablespoons sugar*
¾ *cup heavy cream*
2 *tablespoons slivered*
  almonds

Peel, core and quarter the apples. Cut each quarter into three segments and soak for half an hour in the Calvados.

Preheat the oven to 325°.

Roll out the pastry and use it to line a nine-inch pie pan. Remove the apples from the Calvados, which should be set aside for later use, and arrange them on top of the pastry. Bake in the oven for 30 minutes. Remove and allow to cool slightly. Raise oven temperature to 400°.

Beat together the egg yolks, sugar, cream and reserved Calvados. Pour the mixture over the apples. Scatter the almonds on top and bake for another fifteen minutes in the oven. Serve warm.

4 TO 6 SERVINGS

Glazed Prune Tart

I have often wondered if one of the reasons certain people scorn British cookery is that it makes use of a lot of unfashionable ingredients such as rhubarb, parsnips and turnips. Prunes also fall into this category. I happen to love them but, if I needed any convincing, this recipe, which has recently been appearing on the menus of several good restaurants in England, would convert me.

6 ounces Shortcrust Pastry (see page 64)	1 cup heavy cream
1 pound pitted prunes	⅓ cup sugar
1 cup brandy	4 eggs
	⅔ cup apricot jam

Roll out the pastry and use it to line a nine-inch flan ring. Prick the bottom with a fork and chill in the refrigerator for at least fifteen minutes.

Bring the prunes, brandy and one cup of water to a boil in a small saucepan. Simmer for five minutes and then allow to stand for another five. Drain the prunes and set aside three tablespoons of the brandy water for later use.

Preheat the oven to 350°.

Lay the prunes in concentric circles on the pastry and beat together the cream, sugar and eggs. Pour this mixture over the prunes and bake the tart for 25 to 30 minutes, until the custard has set or a knife inserted into the center comes out clean.

Allow the tart to cool before placing it on a serving plate. Then heat the apricot jam and the three tablespoons of brandy and water in a small saucepan. When it is bubbling, pour it over the tart and serve.

6 SERVINGS

Old-Fashioned Curd Tart

Tea is a particular specialty in the Lake District, and there are literally hundreds of tea shops. But any serious tea taker should make it a point to go and have tea at Rothay Manor Hotel in Ambleside, for Bronwen Nixon, the proprietor and head chef, was chosen Queen of Teas in a nationwide tea competition held some years ago by the British Tourist Authority. It is no mean feat, I need not say, to be so crowned in this kingdom of experts, and the judges declared her tea to be "an almost flawless experience." Mrs. Nixon's scones can be found on page 212; however, she also serves this unusually spicy tart and her Cumberland Rum Nicky (next recipe) for tea although they would more usually be served as desserts. For this reason they are included in this chapter. Serve these wonderful tarts with whipped cream.

6 ounces Shortcrust Pastry
(see page 64)
6 tablespoons unsalted butter
½ cup dark brown sugar
2 eggs
3 ounces cream cheese
½ cup sour cream
⅔ cup seedless raisins
¼ teaspoon allspice
2 tablespoons molasses
Citron or angelica for
decoration

Preheat the oven to 325°.

Roll out the pastry and spread it over a nine-inch flan ring.

Cream the butter and sugar together and beat the eggs into this mixture. Combine the cream cheese and the sour cream and then mix into the butter, sugar and eggs. Stir in the raisins, allspice and molasses. Pour this mixture into the pastry.

Place the tart in the oven and bake for 30 to 40 minutes until the filling is firm to the touch. Allow the tart to cool and then decorate with small pieces of citron or angelica.

6 SERVINGS

Cumberland Rum Nicky

A tart made of dates and ginger, this is a traditional Cumbrian specialty. However, no one makes it better than Bronwen Nixon, who likes to serve it to her guests for tea.

12 *ounces pitted dates,*
   coarsely chopped
   Boiling water
 6 *ounces Shortcrust Pastry*
   (see page 64)
 4 *tablespoons unsalted butter*
 4 *tablespoons dark brown*
   sugar

2 *knobs fresh ginger,*
   scraped and finely chopped
1 *egg yolk, beaten with a*
   little water
2 *tablespoons rum*

Cover the dates with a little boiling water and soak them for half an hour. In the meantime, roll out the pastry and use it to line a nine-inch flan ring. Cream together the butter and the sugar.

Preheat the oven to 350°.

Drain the dates and mix them with the ginger. Spread them over the pastry and dot the top with the creamed butter and sugar. Make strips out of the remaining pastry and place them in lattice strips over the top of the tart. Brush all the exposed pastry with the beaten egg yolk and place the tart in the oven. Bake for 35 minutes. Remove from the oven and allow the tart to cool before removing it from the flan case. Just before serving, trickle the rum over the top of the tart. (This dish is best served warm.)

4 TO 6 SERVINGS

Westmorland Raisin and Nut Pie

Another traditional recipe from the north of England which is frequently to be found on the menu at White Moss House.

PIECRUST

6 tablespoons unsalted butter
6 ounces whole wheat
   biscuits (about twelve
   biscuits)

FILLING

2 cups seedless raisins
½ cup sugar

1 tablespoon cornstarch
¼ teaspoon salt
   Juice of half an orange
   Juice of half a lemon
½ cup chopped walnuts
1 cup heavy cream
2 tablespoons dark rum

Preheat the oven to 400°.

Crush the biscuits into fine crumbs. Melt the butter in a frying pan over very low heat. Stir the crumbs into the butter until blended, then press the mixture into an eight-inch pie pan or flan ring. Bake in the oven for five minutes. Remove and allow to cool.

Cook the raisins in three-quarters of a cup of boiling water for five minutes. (All this part of the recipe can be prepared a day in advance.)

Reheat the raisins if necessary and add the sugar, cornstarch and salt. Cook over low heat until thick, stirring all the time. Remove from heat and add the orange and lemon juice. When the mixture has cooled, add the nuts and pour into the crust. Refrigerate for at least three hours.

Before serving, beat the cream, mix it with the rum and spread on top of the pie.

4 TO 6 SERVINGS

Apricot Bakewell Tart

Bakewell tart was the result of a misunderstanding between Mrs. Greaves, the proprietress of the Rutford Arms at Bakewell in Derbyshire, and her cook. Mrs. Greaves had evidently requested a jam custard tart. However, instead of mixing in the jam with the custard as she was supposed to do, her cook spread the jam on the bottom of the tart. The incorrect tart turned out to be a huge success and today is one of the best-known of all traditional British desserts. This recipe uses apricots instead of strawberry jam, which makes for an interesting and rather unusual variation. It comes from Rosemary Bett, who is not only one of the great cooks of Sussex but was also the first person who made me realize how exciting cooking could be.

6 ounces Shortcrust Pastry
  (see paeg 64)
1 pound apricots, pitted and
  halved (if using dried
  apricots, cook them
  according to the directions
  on the package)
6 tablespoons unsalted butter

6 tablespoons sugar
2 eggs
3 drops almond extract
½ cup flour
4 tablespoons ground
  almonds
½ teaspoon baking powder
1 tablespoon milk

Preheat the oven to 350°.

Roll out the pastry and use it to line a nine-inch flan ring. Prick the bottom with a fork and line the bottom and sides with foil. Fill with some dried beans and bake for approximately eight minutes. Remove the beans and the foil and bake for another three minutes.

Place the apricots on the bottom of the pastry case. Cream together the butter and sugar and then stir in the remaining ingredients. Spread the mixture over the apricots and bake for 25 minutes, until golden.

6 SERVINGS

Almond Fruit Tart

This is another variation of a Bakewell tart which was sent to me by Noreen Hope, one of the hosts of At Home Country Holidays. She has fed many visiting Americans this dessert and reports that it is always received with enthusiasm.

6 *ounces Shortcrust Pastry*
(see page 64)
4 *tablespoons unsalted butter*
4 *tablespoons sugar*
1 *egg*
½ *teaspoon almond extract*
½ *cup ground almonds*

2 *tablespoons apricot jam*
¼ *cup golden seedless raisins*
¼ *cup currants*
2 *tablespoons slivered almonds*
Confectioners' sugar

Preheat the oven to 350°.

Roll out the pastry and use it to line a nine-inch flan ring. Prick the bottom with a fork and line the bottom and the sides with foil. Fill the case with some dried beans and bake for approximately eight minutes. Remove the foil and the beans and bake for another three minutes.

While the pastry case is cooling, cream together the butter and sugar. Beat in the egg, the almond extract and ground almonds.

Spread the jam over the pastry case and sprinkle the raisins and currants over the jam. Spread the butter and sugar mixture over the top and dot with the almond slivers.

Bake in the oven for 35 minutes or until the pie is firm to the touch. Allow to cool and dust with confectioners' sugar.

6 SERVINGS

Ipswich Almond Pudding

Yet another variation on the Bakewell tart, this recipe has no jam and the almond mixture is rather more rich. It is delicious cold and I serve it often on picnics as it is very easy to eat with one's fingers.

8 tablespoons unsalted butter
1/4 cup sugar
2 eggs
1/2 cup heavy cream
2/3 cup ground almonds

2 tablespoons medium-dry sherry
Grated rind of one lemon
6 ounces Shortcrust Pastry (see page 64)

Preheat the oven to 400°.

In a medium bowl, cream together the butter and sugar until light and fluffy. Beat in the eggs and cream, then add the almonds, sherry and grated lemon rind.

Roll out the pastry and fit it into a nine-inch pie pan. Trim the edges and place it on a cookie sheet. Pour the almond filling into the pastry.

Bake in the middle of the oven for fifteen minutes. Reduce the heat to 350° and continue to bake for fifteen to twenty minutes, until the filling is golden brown and firm to the touch. Allow to cool before serving.

6 SERVINGS

Duke of Cambridge Tart

Susanna Heyman Chaffey is an Englishwoman who lives in New York. She recently set up her own catering company specializing in English tarts, called, appropriately, O'Tarts. One of her best is a Duke of Cambridge Tart for which, she tells me, she found the recipe in an old English cookery book. Although it contains no almonds and uses marmalade instead of strawberry jam, this tart, which is rich and translucent, is undoubtedly a member of the Bakewell family. It's best cold with whipped cream.

6 *ounces Shortcrust Pastry*   1 *teaspoon sherry*
    (*see page 64*)   ⅔ *cup sugar*
5 *tablespoons chunky orange*   8 *tablespoons unsalted butter*
    marmalade   3 *egg yolks*

Preheat the oven to 350°.

Roll out the pastry and use it to line an eight-inch flan ring. Prick the bottom with a fork and line the bottom and sides with foil. Fill with some dried beans and bake for approximately eight minutes. Remove the foil and the beans and bake for another three minutes.

Mix the marmalade with the sherry and spread it on the bottom of the pastry. Mix the sugar, butter and egg yolks and cook slowly over gentle heat until the mixture bubbles. Pour it over the marmalade and bake for fifteen minutes, until the filling is firm to the touch.

6 SERVINGS

Eighteenth-Century Lemon Cheesecake

This wonderful recipe comes from Michael Smith, who has transformed an eighteenth-century recipe for cheesecakes into an extremely piquant lemon tart.

6 *ounces Shortcrust Pastry*
  (*see page 64*)

LEMON CHEESE

8 *tablespoons unsalted butter*
8 *tablespoons sugar*
4 *egg yolks*
  Grated rind and juice of
  four lemons

LEMON FILLING

8 *tablespoons sugar*
8 *tablespoons unsalted butter*
1 *cup white breadcrumbs*
3 *eggs*
  Grated rind and juice of
  two lemons
  Confectioners' sugar

Preheat the oven to 350°.

Roll out the pastry and use it to line a flan ring or pie dish that is at least one and a half inches deep and eight or nine inches in diameter. Prick the bottom with a fork, line the bottom and sides with foil and fill with some dried beans. Bake for approximately eight minutes. Remove the foil and the beans and return the pastry to the oven for another two to three minutes.

While the pastry case is cooking, prepare the lemon cheese: Beat together the butter, sugar, egg yolks, grated rind and lemon juice in a bowl over boiling water or in the top of a double boiler until it thickens. Set aside.

To prepare the lemon filling: Beat together the sugar and butter. Stir in the breadcrumbs, eggs, grated rind and lemon juice.

Lower oven temperature to 325°.

Spread the lemon cheese in a layer over the pastry and then cover it with the lemon filling. Bake in the oven for 35 minutes or until the tart has set. Serve while still warm with a little confectioners' sugar sprinkled over the top.

6 TO 8 SERVINGS

Lemon and Almond Tart

This is a very unusual tart that Anthony Pitt serves at Homewood Park. The combination of lemon and almond flavors is extremely subtle; this is a dessert for those who are not enamored of "sweet" desserts. I like to serve it warm.

6 *ounces Shortcrust Pastry*
 (see page 64)
12 *tablespoons unsalted butter*
 1 *cup sugar*
 3 *eggs*
 3 *tablespoons flour*

Grated rind of three
 lemons
1¼ *cups ground almonds*
 2 *lemons, cut into thin*
 slices
 ½ *cup sugar*
 2 *drops vanilla extract*

Preheat the oven to 350°.

Roll out the pastry and fit it into a nine-inch pie pan. Trim the edges of the pastry and place it on a cookie sheet.

Cream together the butter and sugar; beat in the eggs, flour, grated lemon rind and ground almonds. Spoon the mixture into the pastry case and bake for 30 minutes or until the filling is firm to the touch. Remove the tart from the oven and allow to cool.

Place the lemons in a shallow pan and cover with one cup of water. Cook slowly over gentle heat for ten minutes. Remove the lemons with a slotted spoon, taking care not to cut into the flesh. Add the sugar and vanilla extract and boil the juice until it makes a syrup (approximately ten minutes).

Place the lemons on top of the tart and glaze with the sugar syrup.

6 SERVINGS

Sticky Toffee Pudding

Francis Coulson of Sharrow Bay and Shaun Hill have very similar versions of this dessert. It is, incidentally, everything its name suggests. I think of it as *the* pudding for cold winter nights!

4 *tablespoons unsalted butter*
1 *cup sugar*
3 *eggs*
2 *cups flour*
1 *cup pitted dates, coarsely chopped*
1½ *teaspoons baking soda*

SAUCE

1½ *cups heavy cream or condensed milk*
¾ *cup dark brown sugar*
1 *tablespoon molasses*
4 *tablespoons unsalted butter*

Preheat the oven to 350°.

Cream together the butter with the sugar; beat in the eggs and fold in the flour. Measure one and a half cups of water into a saucepan and bring to a boil. Add the dates and simmer for two minutes. Remove from the heat and add the baking soda. Mix into the batter and pour into a well-greased shallow nine-inch square pie pan. Place in the oven and cook for 30 minutes or until set.

While the pudding is cooking, prepare the sauce: Place all the ingredients in a saucepan and bring slowly to a boil, stirring at the same time. Pour a little of the sauce over the sponge, then put it back in the oven for a few minutes to allow the sauce to soak in and bubble. Cut the pudding into squares and serve any remaining sauce on the side.

4 TO 6 SERVINGS

Butterscotch Cream Pie

Another of those sinfully rich, sweet, creamy desserts that have become the trademark of Sharrow Bay. Nouvelle cuisine is not a concept that has touched this hotel, and desserts are Mr. Coulson's particular passion—it is rumored that he uses eight gallons of cream a day in his kitchen.

6 *ounces Shortcrust Pastry*
  (*see page 64*)
8 *tablespoons unsalted butter*
1 *heaping cup brown sugar*
2 *tablespoons flour*

4 *tablespoons cornstarch*
1 *cup condensed milk*
3 *eggs*
½ *cup heavy cream*
  Cinnamon

Preheat the oven to 350°.

Roll out the pastry and use it to line a nine-inch flan ring. Prick the bottom with a fork and line the bottom and sides with foil. Fill with some dried beans and bake for approximately eight minutes. Remove the foil and the beans and bake for another three minutes.

While the pastry case is cooling, melt the butter in a saucepan over gentle heat. Add the sugar and cook until the butter and the sugar form a smooth syrup. Pour in one and a half cups of water and stir until you have a smooth sauce. Remove from the heat and set aside.

In a separate pan mix the flour and the cornstarch with the condensed milk over gentle heat until they become a smooth paste. Add the syrup mixture and continue to cook over gentle heat until thick.

Separate the eggs. Beat the egg yolks and add them to the mixture. Pour the mixture through a sieve into the pastry case and leave to set, about one hour.

Separately beat the egg whites until stiff and the cream till whipped. Mix together and spread over the top of the pie. Sprinkle with cinnamon.

6 SERVINGS

Lemon Sponge Pudding

This is an old-fashioned steamed pudding that can hold its own on any menu. At Michael's Nook, it is served in individual dariole molds. If you wish to prepare it this way, follow the recipe but divide the mixture into six molds rather than putting it all in one bowl and reduce the cooking time to 45 minutes.

12 *tablespoons unsalted butter*	1 *teaspoon baking powder*
¾ *cup sugar*	1 *tablespoon lemon juice*
3 *eggs*	*Grated peel of two lemons*
2 *cups flour*	

Beat the butter and sugar together until light and creamy. Beat the eggs and gradually add them to the butter-sugar mixture. This should be done very slowly or the butter and sugar can curdle. Fold in the flour, baking powder, lemon juice and grated peel.

Place the mixture in a buttered four- or five-cup pudding bowl or six buttered small individual molds and cover with a large piece of aluminum foil that has been pleated down the middle. Fasten it with either string or a rubber band to hold it securely in place. Place the bowl or molds in a large saucepan or a steamer. The bowl or molds should stand on a steamer rack or an inverted saucer and there should be three inches of water in the pan.

Cover and steam for one and one-quarter hours (45 minutes for individual molds), checking from time to time to make sure that the water has not evaporated. If necessary, add more water.

Remove the bowl or molds from the steamer just before serving and remove the cover. Run a knife gently around the edge of the bowl and turn the pudding onto a serving dish.

6 SERVINGS

Marmalade Pudding

Steamed puddings, heavy, fattening and delicious, are such a very British invention. The stodgier ones have largely passed out of favor, but those with a little more sophistication such as Sussex Pond Pudding (which calls for a whole lemon to be coated with a layer of brown sugar and butter and cooked in a case of suet pastry) are still very popular desserts. Marmalade Pudding is another of the more unusual steamed puddings which has survived into the late twentieth century with absolutely no problems. The word *marmalade*, incidentally, has an interesting derivation. It goes all the way back to the Greek word for "honey apple," which was an apple grafted on a quince. The preserve called marmalade was made by boiling originally quince and later any fruit, but particularly tart Seville oranges.

In this recipe, the sponge is cooked in a bain-marie in the oven, which takes less time than steaming and makes for a lighter dessert. The dish is served with a hot marmalade sauce.

8 *tablespoons softened unsalted butter*	*Salt*
	Milk
½ *cup plus 2 tablespoons sugar*	5 *tablespoons orange marmalade*
3 *eggs*	
Grated rind and juice of one orange	MARMALADE SAUCE
1¼ *cups flour*	6 *tablespoons orange marmalade*
2 *teaspoons baking powder*	

Preheat the oven to 400°.

Cream together the butter and sugar in a mixing bowl until they are soft and fluffy. Beat in the eggs and orange rind and juice. Sift the flour with the baking powder and a pinch of salt and fold them into the mixture. Add one or two teaspoons of milk if the batter is too stiff, but it should not be too runny.

Place the marmalade in the bottom of a well-greased English pudding basin or Pyrex bowl that holds at least four cups. Spoon the batter over the marmalade and cover the pudding with a loose-fitting sheet of aluminum foil.

Place the basin in an ovenproof dish or baking pan that contains one inch of water and cook in the oven for approximately 50 minutes or until the sponge has set and the top has turned a light golden color. (A knife inserted into the center will come out clean when the sponge has set.)

Allow the pudding to cool for five minutes, then run a knife around the sides and turn it out onto a serving dish— be sure to scrape out all the marmalade in the bottom of the basin.

To prepare the sauce: Heat the marmalade and six tablespoons of water in a saucepan over gentle heat for about three minutes. Either pour the sauce over the pudding or serve it on the side in a pitcher. Both the pudding and the sauce must be served hot.

4 TO 6 SERVINGS

Treacle Pudding

This remains one of my favorite steamed puddings. In her recipe, Mrs. Beeton points out that a treacle pudding is always popular with children, but I have also rarely met an adult who doesn't succumb to its distinct charm. Serve with heavy cream.

2 tablespoons light corn syrup
2 tablespoons molasses
Juice of half a lemon
1 tablespoon fine breadcrumbs
8 tablespoons unsalted butter,
softened

Grated rind of one lemon
½ cup sugar
2 eggs, beaten
1 cup plus 2 tablespoons flour
1 teaspoon baking powder
Salt
Milk

Mix together the corn syrup, molasses, lemon juice and breadcrumbs. Place them in the bottom of a well-greased English pudding basin or Pyrex bowl that holds at least four cups.

Cream the butter with the grated lemon rind and sugar until fluffy and then add the beaten eggs. Sift the flour, baking powder and a pinch of salt together and stir them into the mixture. Add just enough milk for the batter to drop from the spoon and then transfer the mixture into the pudding basin or bowl.

Cover the basin or bowl with a large sheet of aluminum foil. Make a pleat in the center and tuck it around the sides of the basin. Tie it in place under the rim with a piece of string or two rubber bands. Place the basin on a steamer rack in a large steamer or saucepan, which should be half filled with boiling water. Secure the lid tightly and steam for two hours. Check from time to time to see if the water is evaporating and add more water if the level should be sinking.

To serve: Remove the bowl from the steamer and lift off the foil cover. Run a knife around the pudding and gently turn it out onto a serving plate. Cut into slices and serve.

6 SERVINGS

Christopher Oakes's
Bread and Butter Pudding

I have always liked bread and butter pudding but I was never overwhelmed by it until I tasted Christopher Oakes's version, which he serves at the Castle in Taunton. His is no nursery dish; in his hands bread and butter pudding is transformed into a delicate, puffed-up dessert like a soufflé that suits even the most formal occasion.

4 *eggs*
½ *cup sugar*
1 *teaspoon vanilla extract*
3 *cups milk*
1 *cup heavy cream*
8 *slices buttered French bread*

2 *tablespoons raisins*
2 *tablespoons currants*
Olive oil
4 *tablespoons apricot jam*

Preheat the oven to 300°.

Beat together the eggs, sugar and vanilla extract in a bowl. In a small saucepan, bring the milk and cream to a boil and pour slowly over the egg mixture, stirring while you pour.

Place the buttered bread in an ovenproof soufflé dish. Sprinkle the raisins and currants over the bread and then pour the sauce over all. Place the dish in a pan of water and rub the rim of the dish with a little olive oil to prevent burning. Cook in the oven for approximately 55 minutes or until the pudding is golden brown, has risen considerably and is firm to the touch.

Heat the apricot jam in a saucepan and brush it over the top of the pudding to make a glaze. Serve while still hot.

6 SERVINGS

Baked Pear Pudding

A comforting dessert where the pears are covered with sponge cake. Serve warm with whipped cream or with Orange Custard (see page 155).

4 medium-ripe pears, peeled, cored and cut into eighths	3 eggs
Juice of half a lemon	1 teaspoon vanilla extract
1½ cups half-and-half	⅔ cup flour
¾ cup sugar	2 tablespoons unsalted butter
	¼ cup slivered almonds

Preheat the oven to 425°.

Place the pears in a baking dish and sprinkle the lemon juice over them.

Combine the half-and-half, sugar, eggs and vanilla extract in a blender or food processor. Place the flour in a bowl and gradually stir in the batter mixture. Pour over the pears, dot with butter and scatter the almonds on top.

Cook for 45 minutes or until the top is golden and the pudding is set, when a knife inserted into the center comes out clean.

4 TO 6 SERVINGS

Rhubarb Pudding

Many people underestimate rhubarb. Perhaps because, as Jane Grigson points out in her *Fruit Book*, it comes originally from Siberia, more likely because they have been subjected to old, stringy rhubarb with that overly acidic taste. Rhubarb must be picked when it is young and pink and not when the stems have become thick and green. Being a fan of rhubarb myself, I am always on the lookout for new recipes for it. This rhubarb and bread pudding is my version of a dessert that I was served many years ago at an English friend's house. She then lost the recipe so I was forced, through trial and error, to re-create it as best I could from memory. Serve this pudding warm with whipped cream.

1 *pound rhubarb, cleaned,*   2 *cups half-and-half*
  trimmed and cut into one-   1 *cup milk*
  inch pieces   4 *eggs*
1 *cup dark brown sugar*   1/4 *teaspoon nutmeg*
  Juice of one lemon   2 *tablespoons unsalted butter*
5 *slices "decent" white bread*

Preheat the oven to 300°.

Place the rhubarb in a baking dish and mix it with all but one-quarter of a cup of the brown sugar. Sprinkle the lemon juice over the top. Crumble the bread into small pieces and mix it in with the rhubarb mixture.

Heat the half-and-half and milk in a small saucepan and bring it slowly to the boiling point. In a separate bowl, beat the eggs and gradually pour in the scalded half-and-half and milk, stirring constantly with a wooden spoon. Add the nutmeg and, as soon as the custard starts to thicken, pour it over the rhubarb mixture. Sprinkle the cinnamon and the remaining brown sugar over the top and dot with butter.

Place the dish in a pan filled with enough hot water to

reach halfway up its sides. Cook in the oven for 45 minutes or until the pudding is firm to the touch and the rhubarb is soft.

4 TO 6 SERVINGS

Rhubarb in a Honey and Saffron Custard

The combination of saffron and rhubarb is marvelously imaginative and comes from Joyce Molyneux of the Carved Angel at Dartmouth. Both the colors and the flavor of this dish are extremely subtle and it makes an excellent dessert with which to conclude a rich meal.

½ pound rhubarb
4 tablespoons sugar
8 strands saffron

2½ cups heavy cream
8 egg yolks
3 tablespoons honey

Preheat the oven to 300°.

Clean the rhubarb and cut into half-inch pieces. Divide into six ramekins and sprinkle the sugar over the top. Bake in the oven for fifteen minutes.

While the rhubarb is cooking, pound the saffron with a pestle or with the back of a spoon and place it together with the cream, egg yolks and honey in the top of a double boiler. Cook over simmering water, stirring all the time until the sauce begins to thicken and coats the back of a spoon.

Pour the custard over the rhubarb and set the ramekins in a pan filled with an inch of water. Lower oven temperature to 250° and bake in the oven for fifteen minutes or until the custard is just set.

6 SERVINGS

Peasant Girl with Veil

An aunt of mine used to make this dessert for special occasions. I have no idea about its origins but have always assumed that it was so named because the apples and the breadcrumbs were covered with a "veil" of whipped cream. Made with rhubarb it has rather a sharper flavor, and makes a wonderful cold dessert for a hot summer's night.

1½ *pounds rhubarb* (4 *cups*)
½ *cup sugar*
⅛ *teaspoon nutmeg*
6 *tablespoons unsalted
    butter*
2 *cups fresh breadcrumbs,
    toasted*
1 *cup brown sugar*
1 *cup heavy cream
    Cinnamon*

Wash and trim the rhubarb and cut into one-half-inch pieces. Place, together with sugar and one-quarter cup of water, in a saucepan. Bring to a boil, cover and reduce the heat to low. Cook for about five minutes until the rhubarb is tender but still firm enough to hold its shape. Sprinkle the nutmeg on top and allow to cool.

In a heavy frying pan, melt the butter. Mix together the breadcrumbs and the sugar and add to the butter. Cook over low heat for about four minutes.

In a large glass bowl layer the rhubarb and the crumb mixture alternately, ending with a layer of crumbs. Just before serving, beat the cream until stiff and spread over the top. Sprinkle with cinnamon.

6 SERVINGS

Tipsy Cake

Tipsy cake, so called for its delightfully inebriating potential, was a standard eighteenth-century party dessert. Sometimes also known as Hedgehog on account of its supposed resemblance to that creature, this recipe is the forerunner of that great nineteenth-century dessert, trifle.

1 *homemade sponge cake with jam filling*
1½ *cups sweet white wine or sherry*
½ *cup sliced blanched almonds*

2 *cups Orange Custard (see page 155)*
2 *drops almond extract*
¼ *cup brandy*

Make several holes in the cake with a skewer or knitting needle. Place it on a serving dish or cake stand and gradually pour on the wine or sherry, allowing the liquid to sink into the holes.

Stick the almonds lengthwise into the top of the cake so that they resemble the bristles of a hedgehog. Prepare the Orange Custard and add the almond extract with the Cointreau. While the custard is cooling, pour the brandy over the cake. Once the brandy has soaked into the cake, cover it entirely with the custard. This cake can be prepared ahead of time, but not more than four hours before eating.

4 TO 6 SERVINGS

Frozen Trifle

Here is a contemporary variation on the great Victorian dessert, which substitutes ice cream for custard. It is especially good on hot summer days but, unlike a conventional trifle, it should not be prepared much ahead of time.

3 cups pieces of leftover
   sponge cake
½ cup raspberry jam
¼ cup slivered almonds
¼ cup brandy
½ cup sherry

1 pint vanilla ice cream
1 cup heavy cream
   Citron slices for decoration
6 crystallized violets or
   fresh strawberries

Spread the pieces of cake with the raspberry jam. Be generous. Place the pieces in a glass bowl and sprinkle the almonds on top. Combine the brandy and sherry and pour over the cake mixture.

Remove the ice cream from the freezer and allow it to soften a little before spreading it over the cake and almonds. Place the dish in the freezer until just before serving but do not leave it in the freezer for more than one hour.

Before serving, beat the cream until it is stiff, spread it on top of the ice cream and decorate with the citron slices and the crystallized violets or the strawberries.

4 TO 6 SERVINGS

Blackberry and Red Currant Fool

Fool, originally a synonym for trifle, is an English name dating back to the fifteenth century for a light, unserious little dessert made of clotted cream and crushed berries, among other things. A seventeenth-century description referred to it as a kind of custard, "but more crude, being made of Cream, Yolks of Eggs, Cinnamon, Mace boiled: and served on Sippets [small pieces of toasted bread] with sliced Dates, Sugar and white and red Comfits [preserves] strawed thereon." Oliver Wendell Holmes caught the real meaning of fool when he spoke of its "charming confusion," its "cinnamon and froth."

Gooseberry fool is the English favorite, but any tart berry works. In this recipe, fresh cranberries can be substituted for red currants (should they be too hard to find) to give it the essential sharp taste.

Juice of one orange	*1½ cups sugar*
1 pound blackberries	*2 cups heavy cream*
1 pound red currants	

Place the orange juice, blackberries, red currants and sugar in a heavy saucepan. Cook over the lowest heat possible for five minutes and then purée the mixture in a food processor. Strain through a very fine sieve.

In a separate bowl, beat the cream until stiff and then fold into the blackberry and red currant purée. Place in a glass dish or in individual glasses. Refrigerate for at least three hours before serving.

6 TO 8 SERVINGS

Lemon Mousse

"The days of lemon mousse are over" was the phrase used by one young native hôtelière to characterize the changing gastronomic climate in Britain. I knew exactly what she meant, for when I was growing up lemon mousse was *de rigueur* at every party and festive occasion. A constant diet of lemon mousse would, indeed, become dreary, but I would hate to see it vanish altogether, for it is, whatever else, so reliable, soothing and delicious. It is also one of the easiest of all desserts to prepare for a large number of guests and can be made hours ahead of time. My recipe serves from six to eight people but, for a larger group, double the ingredients. Serve with raspberry sauce on the side.

2 *packets unflavored gelatin*	*Pinch of cream of tartar*
6 *large eggs*	*Pinch of salt*
½ *cup sugar*	1 *cup yogurt*
⅔ *cup lemon juice*	*Fresh mint leaves* or
Grated rind of one lemon	*crystallized violets*

Melt the gelatin in a quarter of a cup of cold water and let it soften. Set the cup in a pan of hot water and stir until the gelatin is fully dissolved.

Separate the eggs and set aside the whites. Place the egg yolks in the top of a double boiler over low heat and beat until they are creamy. Add the sugar, lemon juice and lemon rind, continuing to beat. Stir in the dissolved gelatin and set the saucepan in a bowl of ice cubes. Allow to cool, stirring occasionally until the mixture is thick but not completely set.

Beat the egg whites until they are stiff. Add the cream of tartar and salt and continue to beat until they form stiff peaks.

Stir the yogurt into the lemon mixture. Then fold into the egg whites and transfer to a large glass serving dish. Smooth the top and allow to set for at least three hours. Decorate with a few fresh mint leaves or some crystallized violets immediately before serving.

6 TO 8 SERVINGS

Chilled Mint and Chocolate Soufflé

I met Shaun Hill when he was still the chef at the Lygon Arms in Broadway and had not yet opened his own restaurant. He told me that he had become interested in food after leaving school and not at home, because his mother was in fact a terrible cook. This recipe of his is popular with children who love the color and the taste of the peppermint and its contrast with the chocolate.

5 eggs	1½ cups heavy cream
6 tablespoons sugar	¼ cup honey
½ teaspoon peppermint extract	3 ounces unsweetened dark chocolate
Green food coloring	3 Amaretto cookies
1 packet unflavored gelatin	4 sprigs mint

In a mixing bowl, beat the eggs and sugar together. Add the peppermint extract and enough green food coloring to turn the mixture a very pale green. Dissolve the gelatin in a little boiling water and then add to the egg mixture. (If it should go lumpy, place the bowl in a saucepan that contains a little boiling water and stir over gentle heat until the lumps disappear.)

In a separate bowl beat the cream until it is thick and then fold into the egg mixture. Make collars for four ramekins and then pour the mixture into them. Allow to set for at least one hour in the refrigerator.

Shortly before serving, heat one-quarter cup of water and the honey in a small saucepan and once they have made a syrup, add the chocolate. As soon as the chocolate has melted, remove the saucepan from the heat. Using a sharp knife, cut a plug about one inch deep in the center of each soufflé and remove the top. Divide the chocolate among the soufflés and then replace the caps.

Crush the Amaretto cookies and sprinkle the crumbs on top of each soufflé. Decorate each ramekin with a sprig of mint and serve.

4 SERVINGS

Burnt Cream à l'Orange

Burnt cream, sometimes called Trinity cream since it is believed to have originated in the kitchens of Trinity College, Cambridge, in the eighteenth century, is the English relative and, as far as one can tell, the predecessor of the French dish crème brûlée. This recipe—burnt cream with a difference—comes from Allan Holland, the self-taught perfectionist who has made Mallory Court, near Leamington Spa, worth a detour not only for the comfort of its rooms but for the excellence of its food.

2 *cups heavy cream*　　　　2 *tablespoons Cointreau*
7 *egg yolks*　　　　　　　　　*Grated rind of one orange*
4 *tablespoons sugar*　　　　1 *cup dark brown sugar*

Rinse out a heavy saucepan with cold water and leave wet. Pour in the cream and heat to just below simmering point over low heat.

Meanwhile beat the egg yolks and sugar together until thick and pale in color. Slowly pour the hot cream onto the yolk and sugar mixture, stirring slowly. Then blend in the Cointreau and orange rind.

Rinse out the saucepan and again leave wet. Pour in the custard mixture and over very low heat, or over a pan of simmering water, cook the custard, stirring continuously with a wooden spoon. Make sure, as you stir, that you scrape the entire bottom of the pan. Continue stirring until the mixture has thickened sufficiently (it should leave a trail when you lift out the spoon) but on no account let it boil. Pour the custard into five to seven ramekin dishes (depending on size) and allow to cool. Refrigerate for at least five to six hours or overnight.

One hour before serving, preheat the broiler and place a quarter-inch layer of brown sugar over the top of the custard. Place the ramekins in a baking pan filled with ice cubes and place under the broiler until the sugar melts and caramelizes. (This takes only a few moments.) Remove from the broiler and allow to cool to room temperature but do not place in the refrigerator.

5 TO 7 SERVINGS

Stone Cream

A rich, creamy dessert that appears in many nineteenth-century cookbooks and is probably so called because it resembles the color of stone. A layer of apricot jam is covered with a combination of sherry and lemon juice and then with cream set with gelatin. Traditionally, the cream is heated before being whipped into a mold with the gelatin. However, I find that if it is whipped cold and a beaten egg white is added, it makes for a lighter dessert.

5 *tablespoons apricot jam*	1 *packet unflavored gelatin*
¼ *cup lemon juice*	1 *egg white*
3 *tablespoons sherry*	2 *tablespoons sugar*
2 *cups heavy cream*	6 *sprigs fresh mint*

Spread the apricot jam over the bottom of a medium-sized glass dessert bowl or in five or six individual wine glasses (depending on size). Mix the lemon juice and sherry and pour over the jam.

Beat the cream until it is stiff. Place the gelatin in a cup with a little cold water and let it soften. Then set the cup in a pan of hot water and stir over gentle heat until the gelatin is completely dissolved. Gently stir the dissolved gelatin into the cream. In a separate bowl, beat the egg white until it is stiff and then fold it into the cream. Lastly, fold in the sugar. Spoon the mixture over the jam and sherry and refrigerate for at least two hours before serving. Decorate with sprigs of mint immediately before serving.

5 TO 6 SERVINGS

Flummery

Flummeries have been served in England since Tudor times; the etymology of the word is unknown although it is thought to be Welsh. An early seventeenth-century writer refers to "this small Oat-meal [from which] by oft steeping it in water and cleansing it, and then boyling it to a thicke and stiffe jelly, is made that excellent dish of meat which is so esteemed in the West parts of this Kingdome, which they call Wash-brew, and in Chesheire and Lancasheire they call it Flamerie or Flumerie." The poet Goldsmith referred to a farmer "who used to sup upon wild ducks and flummery." Today it is a dish generally understood to be a kind of white custard jelly often made in an elaborate mold. Here is Michael Smith's recipe. If raspberries are not available, serve the flummery with a fresh orange salad.

2½ cups heavy cream	1 tablespoon rose water
1 packet unflavored gelatin, dissolved in a little water	Grated rind and juice of one lemon
4 tablespoons sugar	1 carton fresh raspberries

Place all the ingredients except the berries in the top of a double boiler over simmering water or into a bowl placed on top of a pan of boiling water. Stir gently but continuously until the sugar and gelatin are completely dissolved.

Pour into four to six ramekins, depending on their size, and allow to cool before placing in the refrigerator to set.

Just before serving, cover the top of each ramekin with fresh raspberries.

4 TO 6 SERVINGS

Gooseberry and Orange Tansy

Tansy is the name of a wild herb that has bright green leaves. Its juice, which is yellow, was thought to contain therapeutic healing powers and in medieval times was used to flavor a great many dishes. Later the word was used to describe foods that had an association with Easter or were yellow in color, such as a tansy omelette. More recently, tansy has come to describe a dish that contains some kind of a fruit purée.

Pamela Godsall, who frequently entertains Americans under the auspices of the At Home program in her fifteenth-century farmhouse at Winsford, Exmoor, Somerset, contributed this recipe. Since gooseberries are so difficult to obtain, rhubarb can be used as a substitute.

4 cups gooseberries or 4 cups
 sliced rhubarb
4 tablespoons unsalted butter
 Grated rind of one orange
3 tablespoons sugar
2 egg yolks

½ cup plus 2 tablespoons
 heavy cream
3 tablespoons fine white
 breadcrumbs
1½ teaspoons lemon juice

Pinch off the ends of the gooseberries and place them or the rhubarb in a saucepan with the butter and grated orange rind. Mash them with a fork over gentle heat and add the sugar.

As soon as they have become soft and mushy, remove from the heat and beat in the egg yolks. Beat the cream until it is thick but not completely stiff and fold into the mixture. Add the breadcrumbs and place the mixture in the top of a double boiler or in a pan over hot water. Heat gently and stir until the mixture is thick. Allow to cool slightly before stirring in the lemon juice. Divide into glasses or individual bowls. Chill for two hours before serving.

4 TO 6 SERVINGS

Peaches with Lemon and Brandy

A simple, quite delicious recipe that was sent to me by George Perry-Smith, whose restaurant, the Riverside in Helford, is held in great respect by many cognoscenti.

10 *large peaches*   4 *lemons*
1¼ *cups sugar*   ¼ *cup brandy*

Skin the peaches by dropping them into a pan of boiling water for one or two minutes. Then transfer to cold water and peel off the skins.

Place the sugar and two and three-quarters cups of water in a shallow pan and boil until a syrup is formed. Cut the lemons into slices (discard the ends) and add them to the syrup. Simmer for ten minutes, then add the peaches and poach until they are tender—test with a fine knife point and lift them out gently as soon as they are cooked. Continue to cook the lemons until the syrup is reduced to half its original amount and the lemon slices begin to look transparent. Allow to cool. Add the brandy to the syrup and the lemons and pour over the peaches.

6 TO 8 SERVINGS

Minted Strawberries

The strawberry season in England is both so short and so intense that great ingenuity has often come into play to devise interesting ways of eating this most popular of all berries. It turns out that strawberries and mint are one of those marriages made in heaven, as demonstrated in this recipe which comes from the Hole in the Wall in Bath.

2½ cups sugar   (approximately two pint
   Vanilla bean   cartons)
 1 pound strawberries   2 tablespoons chopped mint

Make a syrup by boiling together the sugar and three cups of water with the vanilla pod for five minutes. Allow to cool. Discard the vanilla pod.

Clean and hull the strawberries and place in a bowl with the mint. Barely cover with the syrup. Refrigerate for at least six hours before serving.

4 SERVINGS

Strawberry Mille-Feuilles

Pierre Chevillard is the chef at Chewton Glen, a luxurious hotel at New Milton in Hampshire. As his name indicates, he is not British but he is so talented that I cannot resist including this recipe which is his delectable version of strawberry shortcake—layers of fine biscuit filled with strawberries and cream and surrounded by a sauce of crushed strawberries.

5 tablespoons unsalted butter
⅔ cup confectioners' sugar
½ cup flour
1 egg white
   Salt

1 pound strawberries
   (approximately two pint cartons)
2 cups heavy cream
1 tablespoon sugar
   Juice of one lemon

Preheat the oven to 350°.

Melt the butter in a small saucepan and mix in the confectioners' sugar. Add the flour, the egg white (which should not be beaten) and a pinch of salt. Grease two cookie sheets and, using a spatula, shape the mixture into rectangles of approximately two by four inches on the cookie sheets. Spread them as flat as possible. Place the sheets in the oven and bake for six to eight minutes—until the biscuits are crisp and just turning golden. Set aside and allow to cool.

Slice all but six of the strawberries. Beat the cream until it is thick and then spread layers of the strawberries and of the cream between the biscuits, allowing three biscuits per portion and beginning and ending with a layer of biscuit. Place each portion on a separate plate.

To prepare the sauce: Push the remaining strawberries through a sieve together with the sugar and the lemon juice or place all these ingredients for half a minute in a food processor. Pour a little of the sauce around each of the mille-feuilles.

4 TO 6 SERVINGS

Old English Syllabub

This is one traditional dish that has never needed to make a comeback. Syllabub is a name of obscure origin but definitely dates back to Elizabethan times. A middle-seventeenth-century writer suggested his friend "leave the Smutty Ayr of London and com hither . . . wher you may pluck a Rose and drink a Cillibub"; and Davenant (1668) speaks of a certain girl, how

> *Her Elbow small she oft does rub;*
> *Tickled with hope of Sillabub!*

Originally, syllabub was made with warm milk taken straight from the cow and mixed with cider and fruit juice, and everyone seems to have his own recipe for this wonderfully creamy, inebriating dessert. This particular version comes from the Priory Hotel in Bath.

2 *lemons*	2 *cups heavy cream*
2 *oranges*	8 *macaroons*
1 *cup sherry*	10 *roasted almonds*
4 *tablespoons sugar*	

Grate the rind of one of the lemons and one of the oranges on a fine grater and squeeze the juice both from them and from the remaining orange and lemon.

In a mixing bowl, combine the sherry, the orange and lemon zests and juices, sugar and cream. Beat until the mixture thickens and has the consistency of lightly whipped cream.

Take six glass bowls or large wine glasses. Crush the macaroons and place a layer of crushed macaroons on the bottom of each bowl. Using half the whipped cream mixture, divide evenly among the bowls, then cover with a further layer of macaroons and, finally, another layer of cream.

Decorate the top with the roasted almonds.

Chill in the refrigerator for at least two hours before serving.

6 SERVINGS

Orange Syllabub

Most syllabubs contain lemon juice. However, recently I have discovered that a simple orange syllabub is also delicious.

Juice and grated rind of	*2 tablespoons sugar*
2 oranges	*2 cups heavy cream*
½ cup sherry	*Candied orange for*
	decoration

Place the grated rind, orange juice, sherry and sugar in a bowl. Cover and allow to stand in a cool place for at least one hour.

Strain the liquid into a clean bowl and stir in the cream. Beat until the mixture stiffens and makes ribbons.

Place the syllabub in individual wine glasses or small ramekins. Chill in the refrigerator for at least three hours. Decorate with small strips of candied orange immediately before serving.

4 SERVINGS

Port Syllabub

Michael's Nook serves an extremely unusual syllabub which dispenses with fruit juice altogether. It makes for an interesting change.

½ cup port
1¼ cups heavy cream
6 tablespoons sugar

3 egg whites
6 sprigs fresh mint

Using half the port, pour a little into six wine glasses. Combine the remaining port with the cream and sugar and beat until the mixture is stiff and forms soft peaks.

In a separate bowl, beat the egg whites until they are stiff and fold them into the cream mixture. If you have a piping bag, use it to pipe the mixture into the glasses, using a spiral motion until each glass is filled. Otherwise, pile the mixture in with a spoon.

Refrigerate for at least two hours before serving and top each syllabub with a sprig of mint immediately before serving.

6 SERVINGS

Raspberry and Claret Jelly

Jellies were an extremely popular dessert in the seventeenth and eighteenth centuries. In this century they seem to have been relegated to the nursery. However, the right kind of jelly can be both delicious and sophisticated. The following recipe appears regularly on the menu at Homewood Park.

1½ pounds raspberries (pref-
　erably fresh but frozen
　can be substituted)
1 cup plus 3 tablespoons
　sugar

2 packets unflavored
　gelatin
2½ cups red Bordeaux wine
6 sprigs fresh mint
Heavy cream

Set aside ten raspberries and place the remainder with the sugar in a saucepan. Cook over gentle heat for five minutes. Transfer to a food processor or blender and liquidize before passing the resulting purée through a sieve.

Measure out five cups of liquid using whatever amount of water you need to supplement the raspberry juice. Take a little of this liquid, place it in a saucepan with the gelatin and stir over gentle heat until the gelatin is dissolved. Now add the rest of the measured liquid and the wine. Stir for two minutes over heat but do not allow to boil. Pour the liquid into a large glass bowl and allow to set.

Before serving decorate with the whole raspberries and mint leaves. Serve with heavy cream.

6 SERVINGS

Brown Bread Ice Cream

British cooks didn't learn about ice cream until the nineteenth century but after that they made up for lost time; Edwardian cookery books are full of recipes for elaborate water ices, sorbets and cream ices. One of the most popular recipes was brown bread ice cream. It sounds, at first, a bit strange, but don't be put off—the breadcrumbs are crisply toasted and provide a wonderfully unusual contrast with the smooth texture of the ice cream. There are many versions of this recipe. This particular one comes from Pamela Godsall.

1 *cup whole wheat bread-*
  crumbs
6 *tablespoons sugar*
1¼ *cups heavy cream*

½ *teaspoon vanilla extract*
2 *tablespoons confectioners'*
  sugar

Mix the crumbs and sugar together and place in a shallow saucepan. Cook over very gentle heat, stirring frequently, until the crumbs are crisp and toasted. Be careful not to burn. Set aside and allow to cool, breaking up with a fork if necessary.

Beat the cream until thick and fold in the vanilla and the confectioners' sugar. Place the mixture in an ice-cube tray that has dividers removed. Freeze until the mixture begins to harden around the edges (this happens quite quickly).

Remove from the freezer and fold in the crumbs. Return to the freezer and allow to freeze completely before serving.

4 SERVINGS

Gooseberry Ice Cream

Gooseberries are so much more common in Britain than in the States. (I have been told that certain states even have official prohibitions, for some reason, against the cultivation of gooseberry bushes.) All I can say is, seek until ye find them, for they are very special! The natural tartness of the gooseberry makes it an ideal ice cream base. This recipe was sent to me by Imogen Skirving, who, as a member of At Home, frequently entertains Americans. She tells me that this recipe is always a "winner" with her guests.

1 *pound gooseberries*	3 *egg yolks*
(approximately two or	1¼ *cups heavy cream*
three cartons)	1 *teaspoon rose water*
Scant cup sugar	

Place the gooseberries in a saucepan with the sugar and cook over gentle heat until the sugar has melted and the juice has come out of the fruit (the gooseberries should be just beginning to go soft).

Strain through a sieve (reserve the pulp) and place the gooseberry syrup in a pan. Reduce until you have a little more than half a cup of the syrup. Take the gooseberry pulp and liquidize in a food processor or blender.

Pour the syrup onto the egg yolks and beat until the mixture is thick and creamy. Beat the cream until stiff and mix it with the gooseberry purée and the rose water. Fold this mixture into the egg yolks and place in an ice-cube tray that has dividers removed. Place the ice cream in the freezer or an ice cream maker and fully freeze before serving.

4 SERVINGS

Pistachio Ice Cream

This version of the-most-beautiful-to-look-at of all ice creams can be found on the menu at Gravetye Manor, where it is served with a sinfully rich chocolate sauce.

2½ cups milk
⅓ cup Marzipan (see
    following recipe)
    Pinch of salt
6 egg yolks
¾ cup pistachio nuts, ground

CHOCOLATE SAUCE
½ pound dark semisweet
    chocolate
3 tablespoons dark rum
¼ cup heavy cream
2 tablespoons unsalted
    butter

Heat the milk with the marzipan in a small saucepan until it dissolves. Cream the other ingredients together and gradually mix in the milk and marzipan mixture. Place in a bowl over hot water or in the top of a double boiler and cook gently until the mixture coats the back of a wooden spoon. Freeze in an ice cream freezer or pour into an ice-cube tray that has dividers removed and freeze for at least three hours. Stir once or twice during the freezing process.

To prepare the sauce: Melt the chocolate, rum and cream together over gentle heat and stir in the butter. Serve the ice cream on top of the warm sauce.

4 TO 6 SERVINGS

Marzipan

Marzipan, sometimes referred to as marchpane, is another obscure name going back to a Latin original referring to a certain medieval coin. It is a sugary almond paste that was often molded into small ornamental forms, so rich that in Italian it has been known as *pasta regia*. A sixteenth-century text speaks of it as "the meates of denty mouthed persones," and even avers that John the Baptist "hathe preferred wylde honey and locustes to the martspaines and other swete delycates of kynges." It was made, according to a seventeenth-century recipe, "of verie little flower, but greater quantitie of Filberds, Pine Nuts, Pistaces, Almonds and rosed Sugar." Marzipan has also long been used to decorate traditional festive cakes and is always placed between the hard icing and the filling of a Christmas cake.

1¾ *cups confectioners' sugar*	1 *teaspoon vanilla extract*
1¼ *cups ground almonds*	1 *teaspoon lemon juice*
3 *egg yolks*	

Sift the confectioners' sugar and mix it with the almonds. Make a well in the center and add the remaining ingredients. Mix to a stiff dough and form into a ball, kneading the mixture until all the cracks have disappeared.

Marzipan can be stored for up to six months in the refrigerator. However, it must be tightly wrapped in waxed paper or kept in an airtight plastic container; otherwise it will dry out.

1 CUP

Mint Sorbet

Mint is an important ingredient in British cooking. Anyone in the country with even a scrap of earth has some mint growing there. So it is not surprising that many chefs have thought of new and original uses for this aromatic plant. Those whose only experience of mint has been a vinegary sauce drenching a slab of overcooked lamb should try to put this out of their minds and taste instead this delicately flavored sorbet. It is one that is served between courses at Hunstrete House, that exceptionally comfortable and luxurious eighteenth-century manor house hotel near Bristol, well known for its food.

2 cups sugar
1 large bunch fresh mint
1 cup boiling water

Juice of one lemon
Crème de menthe

Combine the sugar with two cups of water in a saucepan. Boil until a syrup has formed, remove from the heat and allow to cool.

Chop the mint and place it in a separate saucepan that contains the boiling water and the lemon juice. Allow the water to cool, then strain off the mint and add the liquid to the syrup. Add a little crème de menthe and, 'if the flavor does not seem sharp enough, add a little more lemon juice. Place in an ice-cube tray that has dividers removed and freeze for at least five hours before serving.

4 TO 6 SERVINGS

Cakes and
Biscuits

H ere are a few recipes that rightfully belong to that best-known of all British gastronomic and social institutions—afternoon tea. I thought I had exhaustively covered the subject in my last book, but how could I not now include Mrs. Nixon's scones and other such delights?

Cakes and Biscuits

Rothay Manor Scones
Bronwen Nixon's Rum
    Butter
Rhubarb Bread
Ginger Biscuits
Bara Brith

Barm Brack
Flapjacks
Hambleton Hall Shortbread
Chocolate Whiskey Cake
Hereford Cider Cake
Mrs. Siddons's Cake

Rothay Manor Scones

Bronwen Nixon's scones demand to be taken seriously. After all, she is the Queen of English teas (see page 167). Scones should be served warm and fresh from the oven. For some reason, they do not keep satisfactorily overnight. Mrs. Nixon serves her scones with rum butter and, needless to say, they are delicious.

2¼ cups flour
  2 teaspoons baking powder
  ⅛ teaspoon salt
  6 tablespoons unsalted
    butter

6 tablespoons sugar
1 egg
2 tablespoons milk, or more
  Rum butter (see next
  recipe)

Preheat the oven to 325°.

Sift the flour and the baking powder into a bowl and mix in the salt. Rub in the butter and add the sugar. Mix the egg and milk together and trickle into the other ingredients, stirring to form a soft dough. If the dough is too dry, add a little more milk. Press the dough into the shape of a cake about one inch deep and place on a well-greased cookie sheet. Lightly crisscross the top with the back of a knife and bake for approximately 20 minutes or until a knife pressed into the center comes out clean.

Take the scone cake off the cookie sheet and allow to cool for ten minutes. Cut into slices as you would cut a cake. Cut each slice in half and spread with rum butter.

6 TO 8 SLICES, OR 12 TO 16 HALF SLICES

Bronwen Nixon's Rum Butter

Rum butter can be kept in the refrigerator for up to three months, and in addition to scones is also delicious with plum pudding.

½ pound unsalted
   butter
1 cup soft light brown sugar

½ teaspoon allspice
½ teaspoon cinnamon
1½ tablespoons dark rum

Cream the butter until fluffy. Add the sugar and beat until light and pale. Beat in the spices and rum. Pack into jars and cover.

APPROXIMATELY 2 CUPS

Rhubarb Bread

This is a tea loaf that contains no yeast. It is quick and simple to prepare. Serve warm, cut into thick slices and spread with butter.

¾ cup dark brown sugar
½ cup milk
⅓ cup vegetable oil
2 eggs
1¼ cups flour
½ teaspoon baking soda

¼ teaspoon salt
¼ teaspoon vanilla extract
1 cup rhubarb, chopped
   into half-inch slices
¼ cup sugar
2 tablespoons unsalted
   butter

Preheat the oven to 350°.
   Combine the sugar, milk and oil in a mixing bowl. Mix in the eggs and then the flour, baking soda, salt, vanilla extract and rhubarb. Mix well.

Pour the mixture into a well-greased 8½- by 4½-inch loaf pan. Sprinkle the sugar over the top and dot with butter. Bake for one hour or until the bread is firm to the touch. Allow to cool for ten minutes and then turn the bread out onto a wire rack to cool completely.

1 LOAF

Ginger Biscuits

Delicious ginger biscuits that can be served with all kinds of desserts. This recipe comes from my friend and earliest cooking mentor, Rosemary Bett, who has been keeping me in recipes for as long as I can remember.

2¼ *cups flour*
    8 *tablespoons unsalted*
      butter
  ½ *cup sugar*
    1 *teaspoon baking soda*

1 *teaspoon ground ginger*
1 *tablespoon light corn*
  syrup

Combine the flour, butter, sugar, baking soda and ginger in a mixing bowl. Add the corn syrup and enough hot water to turn the mixture into a stiff batter (about three teaspoons should be sufficient). Roll the batter into two sausage shapes, wrap them in waxed paper and refrigerate for at least two hours.

Preheat the oven to 325°.

Using a sharp knife, cut each sausage into slices one-quarter of an inch thick and place the slices on two well-greased cookie sheets. Leave a little space between the rounds as they will expand while cooking. Bake in the oven for approximately seven minutes or until the biscuits are a very light golden color.

ABOUT 35 BISCUITS

Bara Brith

This is the name of the famous speckled tea bread which can be found throughout Wales. (*Bara*, in fact, is Welsh for bread.) Unlike scones, this bread does keep well and one Welsh lady I know insists on keeping her Bara Brith sealed in a cake container for at least one full day before she will serve it. Bara Brith should be served with lots of butter. If it does get old and stale, it is still excellent if toasted. This is Bronwen Nixon's version, which she calls Bara Bruth—it is delicious.

3 *ounces fat (half lard, half butter)*	½ *teaspoon mace*
3 *cups flour*	½ *teaspoon cinnamon*
2 *teaspoons baking powder*	⅔ *cup candied fruit peel*
¾ *cup dark brown sugar*	2 *eggs*
Pinch of salt	*Milk*

Preheat the oven to 250°.

Rub the fat into the flour, baking powder, sugar, salt, spices and fruit peel. Beat the eggs and add them to the mixture. Add sufficient milk to give the mixture the consistency of a batter.

Spoon the mixture into a well-greased 8½- by 4½-inch loaf pan and bake for one hour or until a cake tester or knife inserted in the middle comes out clean.

Remove the loaf from the oven and cool for ten minutes before taking the loaf out of the pan. Allow the loaf to cool before cutting it into slices.

1 LOAF

Barm Brack

Possibly the Irish version of Bara Brith? I was given this recipe many years ago by the proprietor of a small tea shop near Worcester who told me that it had originally come from her Irish aunt. Using cold tea as an overnight marinade may seem a trifle unorthodox but in fact this technique or method is used in a number of traditional recipes and, in every case, the end justifies the means.

<table>
<tr><td>¾ cup raisins</td><td>1 cup cold tea</td></tr>
<tr><td>¾ cup golden raisins</td><td>2 cups flour</td></tr>
<tr><td>Grated peel of one lemon</td><td>2 teaspoons baking soda</td></tr>
<tr><td>½ cup dark brown</td><td>¼ teaspoon salt</td></tr>
<tr><td>sugar</td><td>1 egg</td></tr>
</table>

Soak the raisins, grated lemon peel and sugar in the cold tea overnight.

Preheat the oven to 325°.

Sift the flour and mix with the baking soda and salt. Blend in the egg and the tea-and-raisin mixture.

Pour into a well-greased 8½- by 4½-inch loaf pan and bake for one hour or until the loaf is firm to the touch. Allow to cool for ten minutes and then turn out onto a wire rack to cool completely.

1 LOAF

Flapjacks

Flapjacks derive from pancakes or turnovers, as in apple-jacks. They are a traditional English crunchy biscuit, and when I inadvertently left them out of my other book, I received no fewer than three letters drawing my attention to this omission. In an attempt to make amends, here is the recipe.

8 *tablespoons unsalted butter*   *Pinch of salt*
1 *cup plus 2 tablespoons*   2 *cups rolled oats*
   light brown sugar   ¾ *cup cornflakes*
2 *tablespoons light corn*
   syrup

Preheat oven to 300°.

Melt the butter and sugar in a saucepan over low heat. Add all the other ingredients and mix well. Press the mixture with a wooden spoon into a well-greased eight-inch-square baking pan and bake for 35 minutes or until firm and risen.

Allow the flapjacks to cool for five minutes and then cut into squares or fingers with a knife. Allow to fully cool in the refrigerator before cutting through the flapjacks to make slices. Store in an airtight container.

ABOUT 16 FLAPJACKS

Hambleton Hall Shortbread

Those lucky enough to stay at Hambleton Hall are likely to find a small box, containing the most delectable shortbread, stashed away discreetly on a bedside table. I should think midnight starvation rare at Hambleton, for one is fed far too well, but the thoughtfulness of the gesture is typical of the kind of hospitality offered to guests at this hotel. And, indeed, this shortbread is marvelous to nibble on.

1 *cup plus* 3 *tablespoons sugar*
¾ *pound unsalted butter*

3 *cups flour*
1 *cup cornstarch*

In a bowl, place all of the sugar except for two tablespoons together with the butter and cream until light and fluffy. Sift the flour and cornstarch together and mix into the creamed butter. Form the mixture into a ball, wrap in waxed paper and refrigerate for at least one hour.

Preheat the oven to 275°.

Roll out the dough between two sheets of waxed paper to a thickness of one-third of an inch. Cut into rectangles that measure approximately one inch by three inches. Place the slices on a well-greased cookie sheet and bake for 25 minutes, or until the shortbread has turned a very light golden color.

Remove the shortbread from the oven, sprinkle with the remaining sugar and allow to cool before lifting off the cookie sheet and arranging on a plate.

ABOUT 25 PIECES

Chocolate Whiskey Cake

A sinfully rich chocolate cake that comes from Gravetye Manor, where it is served with a coffee sauce.

7 tablespoons sugar
5 egg yolks
3 tablespoons Drambuie
1/3 cup ground almonds
4 egg whites
6 tablespoons flour
1¾ ounces semisweet dark chocolate, grated

FILLING

7 ounces semisweet dark chocolate
6 tablespoons whiskey
6 tablespoons unsalted butter, cut into small pieces
1 cup heavy cream

Coffee Sauce (see page 154)

Preheat the oven to 400°.

Beat the sugar and egg yolks together until light colored and fluffy. Stir in the Drambuie and ground almonds.

In a separate bowl, beat the egg whites until they are stiff. Fold the flour and chocolate into the egg whites and then fold in the egg yolk mixture. Grease two seven-and-a-half-inch-wide cake pans (preferably ones with detachable bases) and divide the cake mixture between them. Bake for eight minutes or until a knife inserted into the cake comes out clean.

To prepare the filling: Melt the chocolate in a saucepan over very gentle heat. Gradually stir in the whiskey, the butter, piece by piece, and the cream. Remove from the heat. It is important not to overcook the filling.

To assemble the cake: Cool the cake halves in their pans for ten minutes before removing them. Place half the cake on a serving dish and spread one-third of the filling over the top. Cover with the other cake half and pour the remaining filling over the top and sides. Allow the icing to set for at least half an hour before serving with Coffee Sauce.

6 SERVINGS

Hereford Cider Cake

I have not included many cake recipes in this book as there were so many in *Great British Cooking: A Well-Kept Secret*. However, I did want to include this version of a Hereford cider cake. No great spectacle, this is simply a very nice, dull cake which is quite content to be subordinate to your morning coffee or afternoon tea.

8 tablespoons unsalted
  butter, softened
½ cup plus 1 tablespoon
  sugar
3 eggs
2¼ cups flour
½ teaspoon baking powder
¼ teaspoon baking soda
¼ teaspoon freshly grated
  nutmeg
⅔ cup country cider
1 tablespoon confectioners'
  sugar

Preheat the oven to 375°.

In a mixing bowl, cream together the butter and sugar until light and fluffy. Add the eggs, one at a time, beating well after each addition. Sift the flour, baking powder and baking soda together and fold them into the creamed butter mixture. Stir in the nutmeg and gradually pour in the cider, stirring.

Grease an eight-inch cake pan, spoon in the batter and bake for 25 minutes or until a cake tester or knife inserted in the center comes out clean. Allow the cake to cool for ten minutes before turning it out onto a wire rack. Sprinkle with confectioners' sugar before serving.

8 SERVINGS

Mrs. Siddons's Cake

Anthony Pitt found this recipe in an old English book and it now appears quite often on the menu at Homewood Park. Since the cake is named for Mrs. Siddons, the famous actress who came from Bath, it seems appropriate that this recipe, which, in fact, is more of a pudding than a conventional cake, should have been resurrected at Homewood, which is just a few miles from Bath.

1½ pounds dried apricots
  1 cup brandy
1¼ cups sugar
  12 ounces Shortcrust Pastry
    (see page 64)
   2 cups Marzipan (see
    page 207)

⅔ cup raisins
¼ teaspoon cinnamon
¼ teaspoon nutmeg
  Grated rind of one lemon
1 egg yolk, beaten
  Sugar

Soak the apricots in a little water for at least three hours. (This step can be done the previous day.)

Place the apricots, brandy and sugar in a saucepan and poach the apricots until soft but not mushy (about fifteen minutes).

Roll out the pastry and use two-thirds of it to line a nine-inch spring form pan. Chill in the refrigerator for fifteen minutes.

Preheat the oven to 350°.

Drain the apricots and spread a layer over the bottom of the pastry. Break up the marzipan into small pieces and dot over the apricots. Sprinkle in some of the raisins, cinnamon, nutmeg and lemon rind. Repeat the layers until the pan is filled.

Place the remaining pastry on top of the cake and flute the edges with a fork. Glaze the pastry with the beaten egg yolk and sprinkle a little sugar on top.

Place the cake in the oven and cook for one hour and fifteen minutes or until the cake is set (when a toothpick inserted into the center comes out clean). Remove the cake from the oven and allow to rest for five minutes before removing the sides of the pan. Glaze the sides with the remaining egg yolk. Cover the top with a round of waxed paper and return it to the oven for another ten minutes so that the sides can lightly brown.

Serve the cake warm.

8 SERVINGS

Hotels and Restaurants Mentioned in the Text

The Carved Angel
2 South Embankment
Dartmouth
South Devon
Tel.: (08043) 2465

The Castle Hotel
Castle Green
Taunton
Somerset
Tel.: (0823) 72671

Chewton Glen Hotel
New Milton
Hampshire
Tel.: (04252) 5341

Ettington Park Hotel
Alderminster (near Stratford-
    upon-Avon)
Warwickshire
Tel.: (0789) 740 740

Gidleigh Park
Chagford
Devon
Tel.: (06473) 2367

Gravetye Manor
Nr. East Grinstead
West Sussex
Tel.: (0342) 810567

Hambleton Hall
Oakham
Rutland
Tel.: (0572) 56991

Hill's Restaurant
3 Greenhill Street
Stratford-upon-Avon
Tel.: (0789) 293563

The Hole in the Wall
16 George Street
Bath
Avon
Tel.: (0225) 25242

Homewood Park
Hinton Charterhouse
Bath
Avon
Tel.: (02122) 2643

Hunstrete House
Hunstrete
Chelwood
Nr. Bristol
Avon
Tel.: (07618) 578

Le Talbooth Restaurant
Dedham
Colchester
Essex
Tel.: (0206) 323150

Mallory Court
Harbury Lane
Tachbrook Mallory
Leamington Spa
Warwickshire
Tel.: (0926) 30214

Michael's Nook
Nr. Ambleside
Cumbria
Tel.: (09665) 496

Milton Sandford
Church Lane
Shinfield
Berkshire
Tel.: (0734) 883783

The Oakley Court Hotel
Water Oakley
Windsor
Berkshire
Tel.: (0628) 74141

The Peat Inn
By Cupar
Fife
Tel.: (033484) 206

The Priory Hotel
Eston Road
Bath
Avon
Tel.: (0225) 331922

The Ritz
Picadilly
London
Tel.: (01) 493 8181

Rothay Manor Hotel
Ambleside
Cumbria
Tel.: (09663) 3605

The Riverside
Helford
Helston
Cornwall
Tel.: (032623) 443

Sharrow Bay Hotel
Lake Ullswater
Penrith
Cumbria
Tel.: (08536) 301

Wheelers Restaurants
25a Lisle Street
London
Tel.: (01) 437 8968

White Moss House
Rydal Water
Grasmere
Cumbria
Tel.: (09665) 295

At Home Country Holidays arranges visits in a small number of country houses including Blunts Chase, Edbrooke House and Langar Hall. For more information contact:

Gretchen Stevens
At Home
Lower House Farm
West Burton
Pulborough
West Sussex
Tel.: (079) 881 800

Index

About the Author

In addition to practicing the art of great British cooking and writing about food, Jane Garmey is an educational film producer. She lives in New York City with her husband and son.